Your ADVENTURES at CERN

PLAY THE HERO AMONG PARTICLES AND A PARTICULAR DINOSAUR!

LETIZIA DIAMANTE
illustrated by Claudia Flandoli

WS Education

NEW JERSEY · LONDON · SINGAPORE · BEIJING · SHANGHAI · HONG KONG · TAIPEI · CHENNAI · TOKYO

PRAISE FOR THE BOOK

"Fun and amusing, but also precise. This book will pique the curiosity of next-generation scientists about CERN. Intriguing and captivating, with jokes to capture the attention of young readers and bring them to the verge of one the largest scientific enterprises ever conceived: the LHC, with its detectors. This book will motivate the young toward science and the achievements of the scientific community."

Lucio Rossi, *Professor of Experimental Physics, University of Milan, Italy (formerly in charge of LHC magnets during the LHC construction and the Leader of the High-Luminosity LHC project at CERN)*

"A clear gap in the market has been filled! This book is informative, well laid out, and easy to read and navigate. It is full of interesting and fun facts with super illustrations about one of the most important scientific research locations on the planet! A must-read for any young and up and coming physicist!"

Doug Ashton, *Key Stage and Science Lead, Kings Norton Primary School, Birmingham, UK*

"Aimed at young people and those who are young at heart, this science-oriented book, with games, quizzes and witty information, is clever and fun!"

Pierre Hantzpergue, *Honorary Professor, University of Lyon, France; Scientific Co-Director of the paleontological excavations in Plagne; and Dinoplagne® Scientific Advisor*

"A fun, fully illustrated book, where every page is a new game and a new incentive to discover what happens in the biggest physics laboratory in Europe!"

Jacopo Pasotti, *Science Journalist, Switzerland*

Contents

Map of CERN
Pages 2–3

Before you begin

Your Adventures at CERN
page 9

Extras

Curiously CERN
A scientific wonderland

CERN is a wonderland for researchers and attracts tourists from all over the world. It was founded in 1954, a few years after World War II, with the idea of building peace through science. It was named CERN from the French name of "*Conseil Européen pour la Recherche Nucléaire*" (European Council for Nuclear Research). Enjoy your visit!

In this book, YOU are the protagonist!

You are about to visit **CERN**, the biggest **particle physics** laboratory **in the world**. You get to decide every move and your choices create the story. To complete the **adventure** successfully, you will need all your intuition and a bit of luck. Solve the puzzles, play the games and discover plenty of curious and fun facts about this **incredible** place.

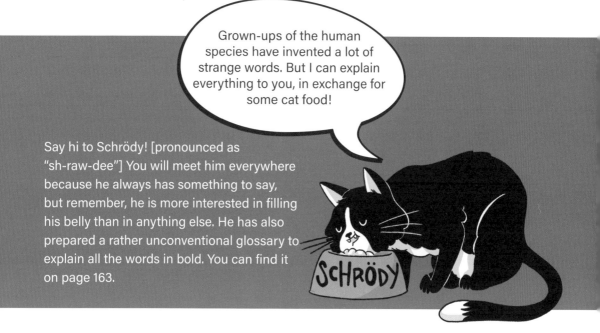

> Grown-ups of the human species have invented a lot of strange words. But I can explain everything to you, in exchange for some cat food!

Say hi to Schrödy! [pronounced as "sh-raw-dee"] You will meet him everywhere because he always has something to say, but remember, he is more interested in filling his belly than in anything else. He has also prepared a rather unconventional glossary to explain all the words in bold. You can find it on page 163.

In this book, you will see how CERN researchers are trying to reveal what happened at the **beginning** of the Universe, almost 14 billion (14, followed by 9 zeros) years ago. You will also explore what's hidden 100 metres **underground**. Yes! You got that right: **a lot** is happening under your feet!

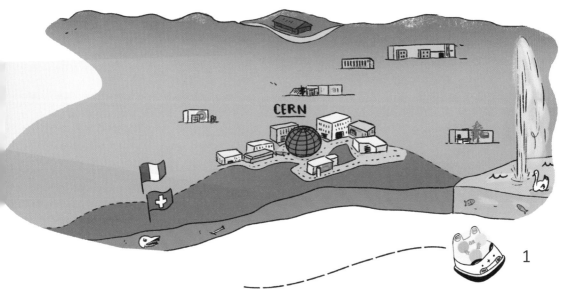

Finding your way around CERN

Before diving in headfirst into the adventure, have a look at this map.

CERN's main site is located right on the border of France and Switzerland, not far from Geneva and its tall water fountain. On the surface nothing looks out of the ordinary, but inside some of these industrial-looking buildings, you can take the elevators to go 100 metres (328 feet) deep under the Earth's surface.

Underground, you'll find:

- a huge circular tunnel that houses CERN's famous **particle accelerator**, or **particle** smasher if you prefer, the **Large Hadron Collider (LHC)**; and

- four big **detectors**: ATLAS detector, ALICE detector, CMS detector and LHCb detector.

Can you spot all of them on the map?

To follow the journey of the **particles**, called **protons**, start from the **hydrogen** canister and follow the black arrows. **Protons** fly around and around at mind-blowing speeds, first inside the small **accelerators** and then in the **LHC**. Their journey ends when they crash against each other inside the **detectors**.

 CERN can be quite a maze! Come back here whenever you need to orient yourself.

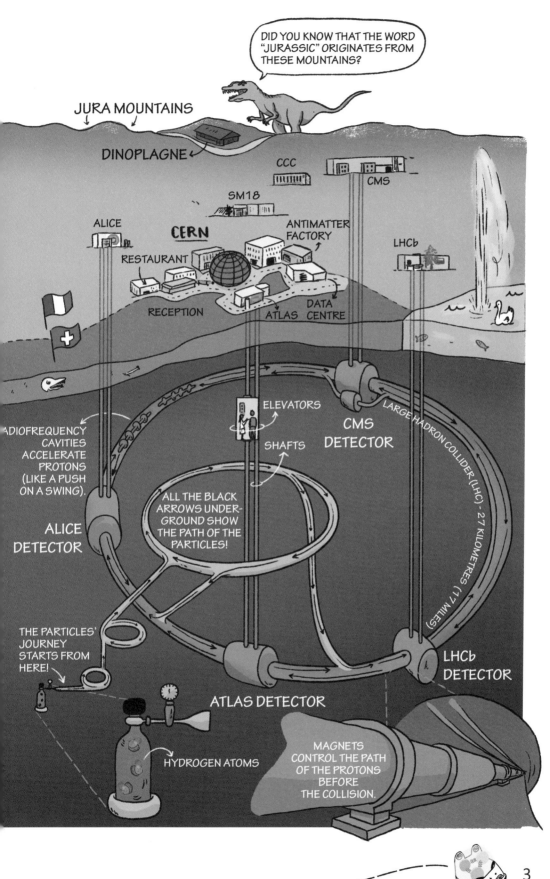

3

Looking inside things

What's the smallest thing you can see? It is probably a bit thinner than a cat whisker. Even if you have eagle eyes, you are still not able to see anything smaller than 0.1 millimetres. If you could, you would see that everything, including yourself, is made of super tiny atoms.

There are more than one million (1, followed by 6 zeros) atoms in the thickness of a kitty whisker. Each atom contains even smaller particles.

Curiously CERN
Itsy-bitsy particles, giant detectors

To study these little itsy-bitsy **particles**, researchers need some of the world's biggest scientific instruments. That's why CERN owns the most powerful **particle accelerator** in the world: the **Large Hadron Collider (LHC)**. This machine speeds up **particles** called **protons** to (almost) the **speed of light**. The goal is not to win a race but to smash **particles** against each other!

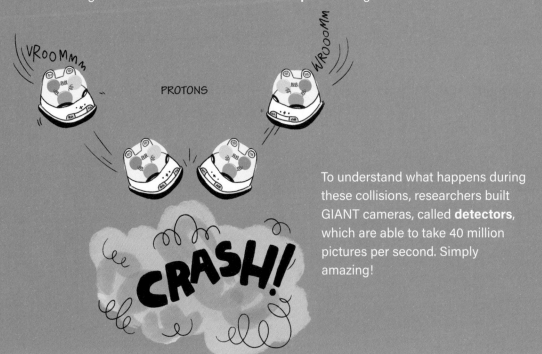

VROOMMM

WROOOMM

PROTONS

CRASH!

To understand what happens during these collisions, researchers built GIANT cameras, called **detectors**, which are able to take 40 million pictures per second. Simply amazing!

Particles you will meet in this book

The **Photon**: It travels at the **speed of light** in a vacuum.

 The **Higgs boson**: Physicists only proved its existence here at CERN in 2012.

The **Electron**: It is responsible for electricity and magnetism.

 The **Muon**: It is the big cousin of the **electron**.

The **Proton**: You will read more about it soon.

And many more!

How small are particles?

Like *Matryoshka* dolls (or Russian dolls), matter can be disassembled into smaller and smaller parts until you reach a piece that you cannot divide any further. This is true for everything that you see around you.

Think about something and ask yourself

"What is it made of?" again and again.

For example, let's start with... Schrödy.

Follow me!

What is a cat made of? A cat is made of various **molecules**, but mainly **molecules** of water.

 What are **molecules** made of? They are made of **atoms**.

  What are **atoms** made of? They are made of a **nucleus** and one or more **electrons**.

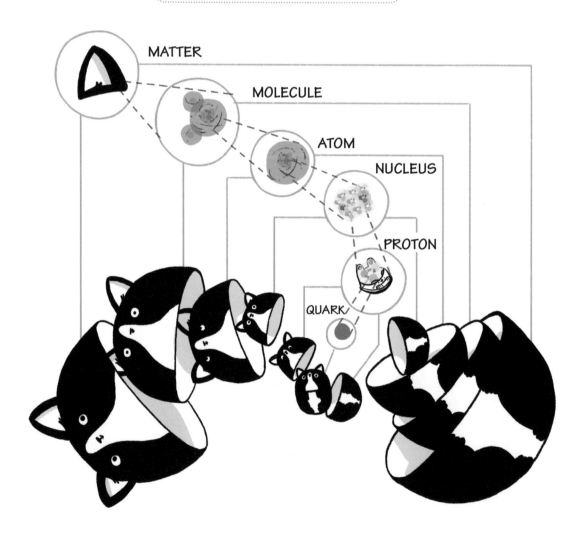

MATTER

MOLECULE

ATOM

NUCLEUS

PROTON

QUARK

What is the **nucleus** made of? It is made of **protons** and **neutrons**.

Ok! Now you can stop because **quarks**, **gluons** and **electrons** cannot be divided any further... at least from what we know.

What are **protons** and **neutrons** made of? They are made of **particles** called **quarks** and **gluons**.

The pictures are not drawn to scale; otherwise, they would be really **gigantic** or ridiculously small. Just to get an idea, enjoy the quiz below.

In a fantasy world of giants

Quiz

If a **proton** was drawn the length of a pen, the smallest **atom** would be as tall as Mount Everest, a virus would be almost as bulky as Earth, and a titbit for cats would take up as much space as _____.

a) the distance between the Sun and Jupiter

b) a kitten

c) the Universe

(Answer on page 150)

Records and surprises

CERN is also the **birthplace** of the **World Wide Web**, which has allowed people to share their ideas, pictures and videos online and across the globe. The **first website** was created **here** more than 30 years ago. This place is full of surprises and there is so much more for you to discover. To warm up, start by answering this quiz:

Curiously CERN

Can you guess which of these Guinness World Records were awarded to CERN?

. . . .

(Hint: There are four correct answers.)

a) The largest scientific instrument

b) The most powerful **particle accelerator**

c) The lowest man-made temperature ever reached

d) The highest man-made temperature ever reached (more than 100,000 times hotter than the centre of the Sun)

e) The first proof of the existence of a **particle** called **Higgs boson**

f) The most international research institute

g) The only place where **particles** cross international borders without passports

h) The production of the fastest **particles**

(Answers on page 150)

You get the idea: this is a place of **SUPERlatives**. Get ready for a thrilling experience, but beware, the adventure you are about to embark on is rather **bizarre**... For there is one small issue— a scary-looking **dinosaur**.

Well, the roars are getting **closer**, and CERN could be in **danger**... Be quick! The adventure has already begun!

Who would you like to be?

First, choose who you would like to be. The options are:

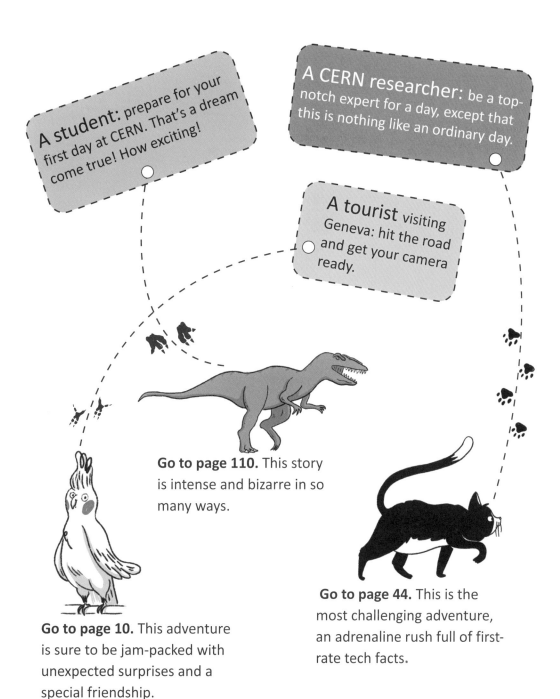

A student: prepare for your first day at CERN. That's a dream come true! How exciting!

A CERN researcher: be a top-notch expert for a day, except that this is nothing like an ordinary day.

A tourist visiting Geneva: hit the road and get your camera ready.

Go to page 110. This story is intense and bizarre in so many ways.

Go to page 10. This adventure is sure to be jam-packed with unexpected surprises and a special friendship.

Go to page 44. This is the most challenging adventure, an adrenaline rush full of first-rate tech facts.

If you choose to be a tourist in Geneva...

A vivid blue sky and a stunning view of the **Alps—Europe's biggest mountain range**—doused in sunlight welcome you to Geneva. It is a beautiful winter's day. You can see up to the magical snow-capped peak of **Mont Blanc**, Europe's highest mountain and beloved destination for ski lovers.

It is your first time in **Switzerland**. You cannot wait to walk around **Lake Geneva** (or *le Léman*, as the locals call it), explore one of the most multicultural cities in the country, and taste a tonne of delicious **Swiss** chocolate. You also check the time on a big flower clock.

Enjoy the scenery as much as you can, but you should know that things will soon get messy. To overcome some hurdles along the way, you need to make two extremely crucial decisions now.

Choose your helper

The helper will be important when you face unexpected tricky situations. You have three options, but only one of them will be essential for your mission. Follow your instinct and pick one.

○ CERN firefighter

○ A travel agent

○ A magician

Choose your tool

You never know what awaits you... At a certain point in your adventure, you will need one of these items, but which one? Take a guess and keep your fingers crossed.

○ A shopping bag full of groceries

○ A bag of bird seeds

○ A pair of binoculars

Tip: Put a tick next to your choices!

Now turn the page and
good luck! 🍀

I know the travel agent. She always gives me tasty treats!

11

You have a sweet little pet bird that follows you **everywhere**, flying no more than a metre above your head. Both of you are **inseparable** and you never leave home without him. For generations, your family has had a strong tradition of taming cockatiels and naming them "**Cheepy**".

You have a lot of **sightseeing** activities planned for today. Certainly, you cannot leave Geneva without appreciating the splendour of the **Palace of Nations** (*Palais des Nations* in French), the home of the United Nations Office. Here, diplomats and country representatives from the **four corners** of the world negotiate the most delicate international issues and discuss human rights.

Cheepy's presence might **raise** a lot of eyebrows, so you muss your hair a bit to create a snug, temporary **nest** for your pet and place your big hat on top. **Hidden** there, he looks and breathes through the coarse wool knitting of your hat. The bird enjoys the view from this unusual position, and nobody can notice his presence.

"Cheepy, are you comfy up there?" you ask **discreetly**.

"*Cheep-cheep,*" says Cheepy. You know that means "yes" in bird language.

Cockatiels often learn to speak and whistle, and Cheepy's parents could easily **mimic** human voices. Cheepy, however, does not seem to take after his parents despite all your efforts and patience. Anyway, Cheepy is your beloved pet, and you like him just as he is.

Your second destination for today is the **Natural History Museum of Geneva** (or *Muséum d'histoire naturelle de Genève* in French). This is Switzerland's **largest** museum of its kind and contains the world's biggest collection of books about bats. It also hosts Janus, the oldest **two-headed** turtle.

As you get ready to enter, you accommodate Cheepy on your head, **hidden** under your hat. You begin the visit, starting from the room dedicated to the **local fauna**. Cheepy moves his head around, feeling **disconcerted**. He is really confused by the fact that all these stuffed animals, such as the Alpine ibex and marmots, do not move a muscle or emit a single sound.

Next, you turn your attention to the **exotic** animals. A few steps ahead, you see eight aggressive tigers gathered in a semi-circle. They seem ready to **pounce** on you at any moment, and you feel Cheepy **trembling** under your hat. These **huge** felines make your friend—who gets frightened even by cute, harmless kittens—break out in a cold sweat. Better get out of here. Passing in front of a replica of a **T-Rex** skull, you hurry towards an animal that looks like a small ostrich.

"Look, Cheepy, this is a **Kangaroo Island emu**. It says that this is the **only** known specimen in the world," you point out. Your friend relaxes a little, but he gets very sad when he realises how many animals have become extinct.

Science Byte

Saving animals in the wild

Dinosaurs, woolly mammoths and sabre-toothed cats went extinct long ago, but a lot of animals disappear or are threatened with extinction every year. For example, the West African black rhinoceros were declared extinct in 2011, and all five of the world's river dolphin species are at risk. The Kangaroo Island emu (*Émeu de Baudin* in French) was discovered at the beginning of the 1800s and declared extinct after less than 30 years, most likely because it was heavily hunted and its habitat was destroyed. The eight stuffed tigers in the Museum belong to eight different subspecies of tigers, of which two have gone extinct. The Museum also displays three bearded vultures, which are huge birds of prey with a wingspan of up to three metres (9.8 feet). Hunters completely wiped them out from the Alps. They could not be seen in these mountains for almost a century, but they were recently reintroduced.

You advance to page 100.

It is an extremely dangerous jump, but luckily, both of you manage to open the parachute at the right time and land without breaking any bones.

The **massive** ALICE **detector** is in front of you with its characteristic red doors. **ALICE** stands for <u>A</u> <u>L</u>arge <u>I</u>on <u>C</u>ollider <u>E</u>xperiment, and you take a second to admire it. Each red door weighs 350 tonnes and the entire **detector** a **whopping** 10,000 tonnes, the equivalent of 2000 African elephants. It is as **long** as 6 Nile crocodiles (26 metres) and as **high** as 3 giraffes standing one on top of another (16 metres). You cannot resist taking a photo.

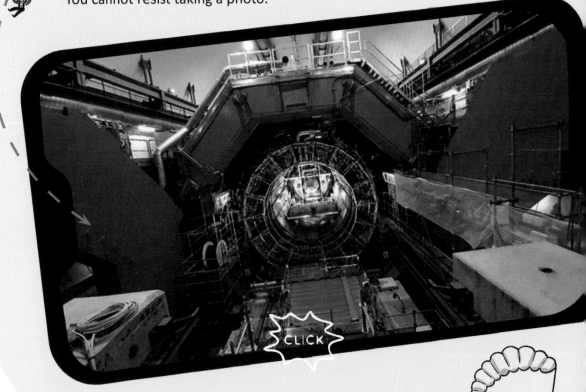

CLICK

"Moooove!!!," shrieks Mr Hacktosis. You are thankful for the fact that he keeps on using **one-syllable** words to communicate with you, so his stinky breath is more bearable.

ALICE's hot soup

Do you remember that everything around us can be deconstructed into smaller parts, like a *Matryoshka* (or Russian) doll, until we reach the small elementary **particles**? (See page 6.) Researchers at ALICE study the type of matter that existed billions of years ago, long before the origin of planets, galaxies and stars. Those days, at the beginning of the Universe, elementary **particles** were unbound or not yet assembled into anything.

Hundreds of seconds after the **Big Bang**, it was too hot for **electrons** to join atomic **nuclei** to make **atoms**. **Quarks** and **gluons** could not stick together to form **protons** and **neutrons**. The Universe was nothing but a hot and dense soup of **particles**: the so-called primordial soup.

Since we cannot go back in time to have a look at this soup, ALICE researchers try to recreate it using **particle** collisions at very high energy and temperatures.

In ALICE, **particle** collisions generate (within a very tiny volume) temperatures which are much higher than those in the heart of the Sun!

Can you add some fish to the soup?

Quiz

Cook the hot primordial soup

You have **hydrogen atoms**, water **molecules**, a mix of free **quarks**, **gluons** and **electrons**, and a box of vegetables. Only one of them is the right ingredient for the primordial soup. Which one is it?

(Answer on page 152)

 Once you have "cooked" your soup, go to page 85.

go to page 85.

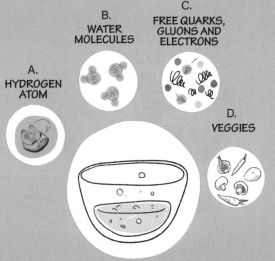

A. HYDROGEN ATOM

B. WATER MOLECULES

C. FREE QUARKS, GLUONS AND ELECTRONS

D. VEGGIES

ARTISTIC INTERPRETATION OF THE PRIMORDIAL SOUP

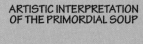

ELENA is the name of a decelerator inside CERN's antimatter factory. It stands for Extra Low Energy Antiproton ring. Prof. Virtualli must have hidden another letter of the password on a piece of paper near ELENA and bound it with a steel paperclip. That's the secret message in Prof. Virtualli's poetry. You dart there in a blink of an eye.

Curiously CERN

What are antiprotons?

While **protons** are flying faster and faster inside the **LHC**, ELENA actually has the opposite goal: it is used to reduce the speed of the **particles** (in this case, **antiparticles**). That's why it is a decelerator and not an **accelerator**. While **protons** fly inside the **LHC**, **ELENA** works with anti**protons**, which are like **protons**, but with the opposite **charge**.

PROTON

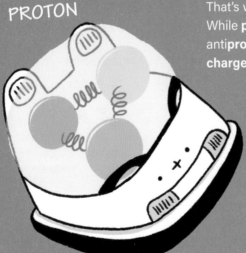

ANTIPROTON

As soon as you reach ELENA, the **decelerator ring**, you find a wooden stick, a long piece of string, and a **magnet** shaped like a ring.

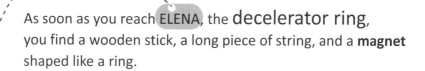

Find these items in the picture of ELENA:

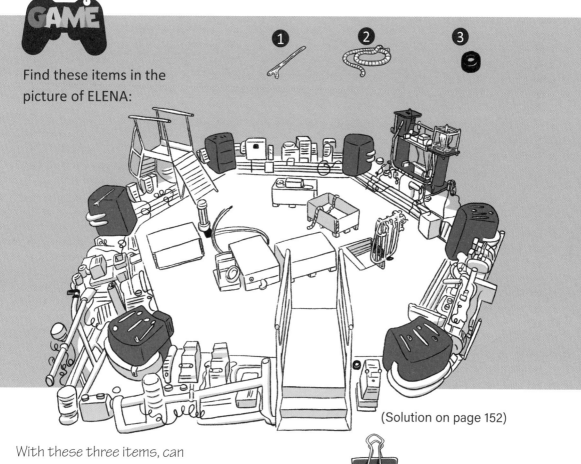

(Solution on page 152)

With these three items, can you construct something to fish up the piece of paper bound by the steel paperclip? Draw your idea in the space provided.

Once you are done, go to page 30 to see how the drawing compares with yours.

Without the glass of water, your only option is to grab a **bicycle** and cycle as fast as possible along the tunnel towards the ATLAS **detector**.

Unfortunately, one of the tyres is **almost flat**, which means that cycling becomes tougher and tougher. In the meantime, Mr Hacktosis also jumps on a bicycle. While you are **gasping** for breath, he cycles ahead and finds the **last piece** of the password. Sorry to say, but for you, it is **game over**.

It is better to choose the glass of water. Look for one and find a smart way to use it on page 77.

THE LHC IS VERY LOOOONG. PEOPLE WHO CHECK AND REPAIR THE LHC CAN USE BICYCLES TO TRAVEL ALONG THE TUNNEL.

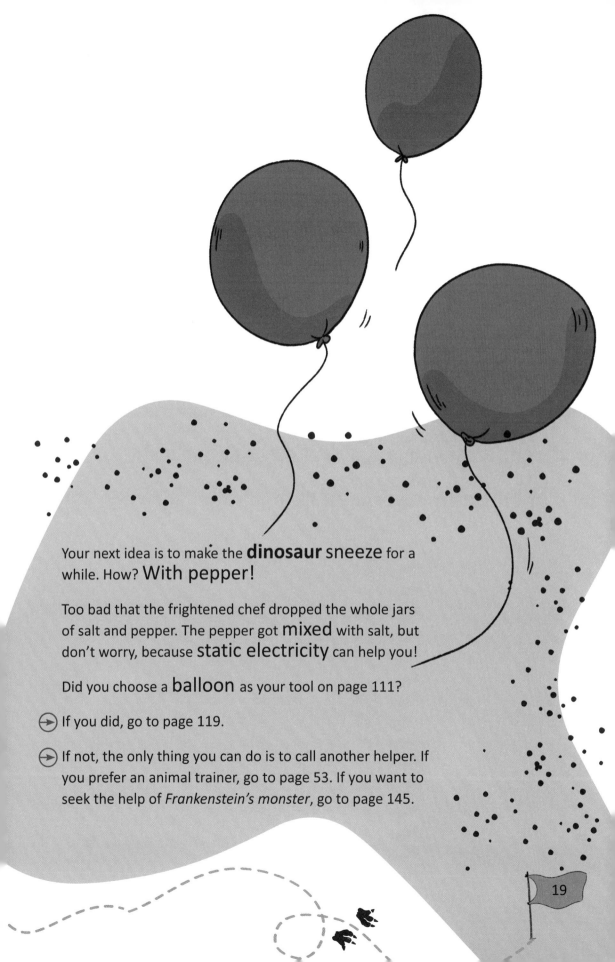

Your next idea is to make the **dinosaur** sneeze for a while. How? With pepper!

Too bad that the frightened chef dropped the whole jars of salt and pepper. The pepper got mixed with salt, but don't worry, because static electricity can help you!

Did you choose a **balloon** as your tool on page 111?

→ If you did, go to page 119.

→ If not, the only thing you can do is to call another helper. If you prefer an animal trainer, go to page 53. If you want to seek the help of *Frankenstein's monster*, go to page 145.

Better not to tell Schrödy

The words **electron**, electricity and electric come from "*elektron*", which means amber in ancient Greek, but why? The ancient Greek Thales of Miletus (624–545 BC) found out about static electricity by rubbing a piece of fossil tree resin, called amber, with some fur (likely cat's fur). He did not know about **electrons**, but he had fun using the amber stone with the electrostatic **charge** to attract feathers. Beyond that, amber is also an excellent material for preserving **dinosaurs**! Did you know that a 99-million-year-old **dinosaur** tail was found inside a piece of amber in Myanmar?

WRAAAA

When you've collected enough pepper, you **throw** it towards the **dinosaur**, hoping that it will trigger some sneezing.

However, pepper is not making a dent. **Undaunted**, the **dinosaur** continues to roar and generate panic around the campus.

20

You should choose another helper on page 134.

You have found **five letters** so far: H, E, C, P, and Y. You can form different passwords with these five letters, such as EPCYH or HECYP.

But let's start with something simpler:

Step 1 - If the password had just two letters (for example H and E), you could arrange them only in two ways: HE or EH. (It is also: 2x1=2)

Step 2 - If the password had three letters (H, E and P), you could arrange them in six ways: HEP, HPE, EHP, EPH, PEH, PHE. (It is also: 3x2x1=6)

Quiz

Step 3 - How many combinations can you have with four letters (H, E, P and Y)?

a) 24

b) 8

c) 22

(Hint: You can try to write all the combinations for these four letters, like HEPY, HEYP, HPEY and so on, in the table below; or you can use the mathematical trick shown in the previous examples. In this case, it would be: 4x3x2x1. Go to page 153 to check if you have all the possible combinations.)

HEPY	HEYP	HPEY			

With the five letters that you have collected (H, E, C, P, Y), you have **120** (that's **5x4x3x2x1**) possible passwords.

Step 4 - On top of that, you are still short of the **sixth** letter, which you could not find inside the **antimatter** factory. If you had it, you would have **720** options. But since the letter is missing, it could be **any** of the 26 letters of the English alphabet from A to Z. Basically, it means that you have 720 possibilities **multiplied** by 26, which gives you **18,720** possible passwords! Your brain is **burning**, and your **confidence** is fading. Goodness gracious...

Let's see what happens on page 124.

Since your first idea is not feasible, you come up with another idea. "Can **dinosaurs** get drunk on champagne?" you wonder. Your imagination knows no boundaries.

Did you choose champagne as your tool on page 111?

➡ If you did, go to page 143.

➡ If not, go to page 123.

Unaware of the flipped arrow, Mr Hacktosis cycles all the way to the CMS **detector.** When he arrives, the police are there waiting for him. Ha ha ha, serves him right!

In the meantime, you find the remaining piece of the password between the ALICE and ATLAS **detectors.** The letter is hidden in a weird-looking sentence. Play the game to find out.

Follow the hidden clue

The letters of each word have been swapped following a certain rule. Figure the rule and you're golden.

Eakt eht dhirt rettel fo eht dorw shysicp.

(Hint: Look at the first and last letters of each word in this sentence.

Solution on page 153)

Now you are ready to continue your adventure. The letter box below contains the key to your next move.

Letter box

Circle the following words in the word search. The remaining letters from top to bottom will tell you where to go next.

- PARTICLE
- ATLAS
- CMS
- LHCB
- PROTON
- ACCELERATOR
- ALICE
- MAGNET
- PHYSICS
- DETECTOR
- PENGUIN
- PETA
- QUARK
- GLUON
- SOUP
- ELECTRON
- CAT
- DINOSAUR

A	T	L	A	S	T	Q	R	G	N	O
T	C	T	O	E	O	U	U	O	P	A
G	E	C	N	P	A	U	R	A	E	T
P	W	G	E	S	H	T	P	R	R	E
P	A	A	O	L	C	Y	O	C	L	K
M	E	N	L	E	E	T	S	C	M	N
G	I	N	L	I	C	R	I	I	O	S
D	L	E	G	E	C	T	A	T	C	B
C	E	U	T	U	R	E	O	T	C	S
N	A	E	O	A	I	R	T	H	O	Y
O	D	T	P	N	P	N	L	N	E	R

 G_ T_ P___ T_____-___.

(Solution on page 152)

You are almost falling off the crane, and a **firefighter** comes to your rescue. During the desperate attempt to save Cheepy, your phone **crashes** on the floor and the camera **breaks.** That's too bad, but at least you are still alive and the firefighter helps both you and Cheepy to come down safely. Phew... you heave a sigh of relief!

You are thanking the firefighter, when a **loud din** of birds pervades the workshop area. Cheepy gives you a horrified look and **swoops** through the main door. "Cheepy, where are you going now?" you shout, baffled.

"Your bird should not worry. This is just an **audio recording** of birds of **prey,** which is played regularly in the building to prevent pigeons and other local birds from entering and leaving their droppings on these **precious** big **magnets**," says the firefighter. But Cheepy flew away without hearing a single word of the firefighter's explanation.

Where is Cheepy going? Quick, follow him to page 146.

24

You put a **full** glass of water in front of the arrow sign. When you look at it, you see that the glass of water **flips** the direction of the arrow. What a wonderful trick!

Flipping arrows

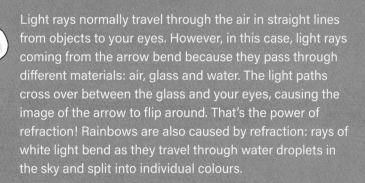

ATLAS

ATLAS

ATLAS

Light rays normally travel through the air in straight lines from objects to your eyes. However, in this case, light rays coming from the arrow bend because they pass through different materials: air, glass and water. The light paths cross over between the glass and your eyes, causing the image of the arrow to flip around. That's the power of refraction! Rainbows are also caused by refraction: rays of white light bend as they travel through water droplets in the sky and split into individual colours.

Mr Hacktosis turns to the **wrong** direction. He thinks he's going from ALICE towards the ATLAS **detector**, but actually, he's running towards the CMS **detector** (see the position of the **detectors** on page 3).

Curiously CERN

CMS and its smashing success

CMS means Compact **Muon** Solenoid. The entire **detector** is 21 metres long (as long as a train carriage) and 15 metres high, which is like an unimaginable tower of three giraffes, standing one on top of another.

CMS is the heaviest **LHC** experiment: it weighs 14,000 tonnes; that is more than a huge herd of 2800 African elephants. It contains a spiral-shaped **magnet**, which is also the heaviest **magnet** in the world.

Researchers working at both the CMS and ATLAS experiments discovered a new **particle** called **Higgs boson** in 2012. That was a smashing success because proving the existence of this **particle** had been a researchers' dream for many years.

Great, he has **fallen** for your trick! Now that you are off the hook, you can call the **police.**

Make your way to pages 80–81.

Three, two, one, GO!

Just for fun, let's compare the **speed of light** with the fastest human being, the speediest animals and the quickest forms of transport:

Go!

KMPH = KILOMETRES PER HOUR
KMPS = KILOMETRES PER SECOND

MPH = MILES PER HOUR
MPS = MILES PER SECOND

THE JAMAICAN RUNNER USAIN BOLT BROKE THE WORLD RECORD. HIS AVERAGE SPEED IS 37.57 KMPH (23.34 MPH).

8

PASSENGER AIRCRAFT FLY AT ABOUT 930 KMPH (570 MPH). 3

4

CURRENTLY, THE FASTEST TRAIN IS THE SHANGHAI MAGLEV (SHORT FOR MAGNETIC LEVITATION). IT RUNS AT ABOUT 430 KMPH (267 MPH).

THE SPEEDIEST DINOSAURS WERE THE ORNITHOMIMIDS. THEY COULD PROBABLY RUN AT SPEEDS OF UP TO 60 KMPH (37 MPH).

7

THE PEREGRINE FALCON IS THE FASTEST BIRD. IT HAS A DIVING SPEED OF 389 KMPH (242 MPH). 5

CHEETAHS ARE THE FASTEST ANIMALS ON LAND: 96.6 KMPH (60 MPH).

6

A SPACE SHUTTLE MUST REACH SPEEDS OF ABOUT 28,000 KMPH (17,500 MPH) TO REMAIN IN ORBIT. 2

THE SPEED OF LIGHT IS ABOUT 1,000,000,000 KMPH (670,000,000 MPH), BUT IT IS USUALLY EXPRESSED AS ABOUT 300,000 KMPS (186,000 MPS). 1

Photons (light **particles**) can fly from Earth to the Moon in around 1 second. **Protons** flying inside the **Large Hadron Collider (LHC)** at CERN are almost as fast: they reach 99.9999991% the **speed of light**. Wow, that figure sure has a lot of nines!

"Think of the **LHC** as a racing circuit with two-way traffic," explains Marta. "The **protons** are like little bumper cars speeding around the circuit until they hit each other."

"We want these bumper cars to collide head-on at a few crossing points in the **LHC** ring where the giant **detectors** are located. These are: the ALICE, ATLAS, CMS and LHCb **detectors**," she continues.

(You can refer to the map on pages 2–3 to locate the four **detectors**.)

"However, **particle** collisions are very different from the collisions that happen in our daily lives. This may sound crazy to you, but rather than disintegrating into thousands of pieces, when these **protons** smash together, they transform into other **particles**. For instance..."

Marta pauses for a few seconds, then comes up with a really mind-blowing analogy. "It would be like two bumper cars crashing and transforming into a boat, a bicycle and a helicopter. In another bumper car crash, however, a cruise ship pops out from the collision. Do you get the idea?"

The visitors look quite perplexed.

"The world of **particle physics** is really bizarre, but I love studying it," she adds.

I can run around 48 kilometres per hour (30 miles per hour), which is 0.01 kilometres per second (0.006 miles per second). What about you? Can you catch me?

Turn the page to see two examples of **proton-proton** collisions.

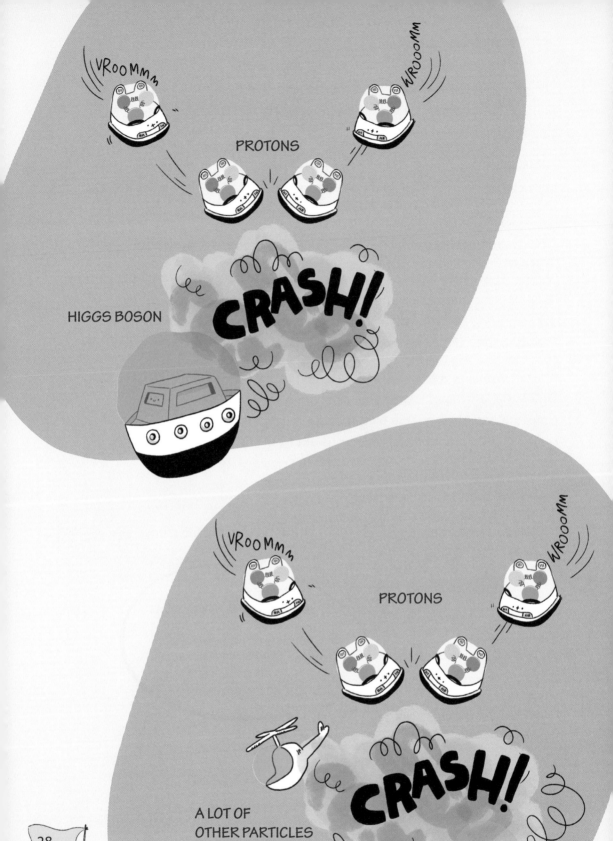

During the guided tour, you realise that all the roads at CERN are named after famous **physicists**. You are currently walking along *Route W. Pauli,* or W. Pauli street, which was named after **Wolfgang Pauli** (1900–1958).

Who was Wolfgang Pauli?

He was one of the superstars of **quantum physics** and received the **Nobel Prize** in Physics in 1945. He discovered that some **particles**, like **electrons**, cannot be at the same place at the same time, with the same energy.

Funny anecdote: It is said that when Wolfgang happened to stand near some experimental equipment, it would self-destruct. Such a weird phenomenon happened quite often apparently and got the name "Pauli Effect"!

Wolfgang is known for a comment he made, which sounds confusing but very profound: "This isn't right. This isn't even wrong." He referred to a scientific claim that could not be proven. For example, you can say: "Mammals do not lay eggs," and then you can travel around the world to verify if it is true or not. As soon as you or someone else finds an example of a mammal that lays eggs, such as the duck-billed platypus in Australia, you know that your claim was false. However, if you declare something that cannot be tested (at the moment, at least), like: "Aliens live on planet Mercury and speak English," nobody can demonstrate if it's right or wrong.

> I always blame the Pauli Effect when things around me break apart.

> This isn't right. This isn't even wrong.

This photo shows Wolfgang Pauli and another famous physicist, Niels Bohr, exploring the physics of a spinning top. Maybe it was their favourite toy, and how can we blame them?

Follow the tour to page 82.

You can use the **magnet**, the stick and the string to construct a fishing rod, like the one below, then try to attract the paperclip that has a sheet of paper bound to it.

You fish far and wide and start pulling up all sorts of forgotten magnetic objects.

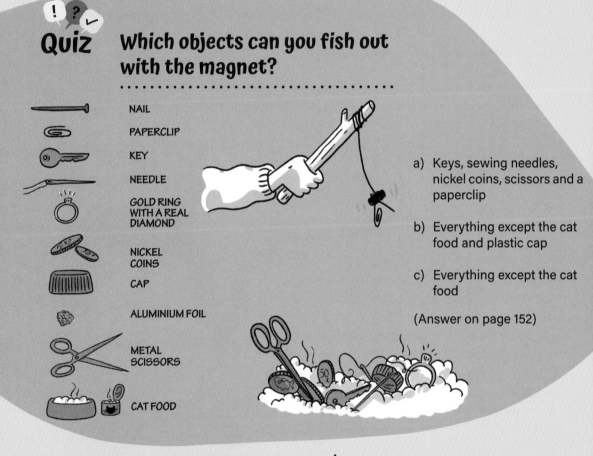

QUIZ

Which objects can you fish out with the magnet?

NAIL

PAPERCLIP

KEY

NEEDLE

GOLD RING WITH A REAL DIAMOND

NICKEL COINS

CAP

ALUMINIUM FOIL

METAL SCISSORS

CAT FOOD

a) Keys, sewing needles, nickel coins, scissors and a paperclip

b) Everything except the cat food and plastic cap

c) Everything except the cat food

(Answer on page 152)

You find a paperclip, but there is **no sign** of the piece of paper which was **supposed** to come together with it.

Did someone take the fourth piece of the password before your arrival?

That would be a **tragedy!** But you do not give up and decide to get the other letters of the password as quickly as possible.

30

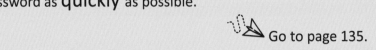
Go to page 135.

Cheepy is not easy to spot with the naked eye, but binoculars can help.

You look around restlessly until you spot your friend in the horizon. He flew past the water tower and is heading towards a big building called **Building 180**.

Great! You decide to drive the double-decker bus there.

Turn the page.

You end up inside Building 180. It is a big workshop area where the **magnets** for the **LHC** are produced and tested.

Find the LHC magnets
. . . .

The **LHC magnets** under construction have not been coated in blue yet. There are five of them in this picture. Can you spot them? (Solution on page 154)

But where is Cheepy and the unstoppable cat? Your binoculars come in handy once again...

You search high and low to page 41.

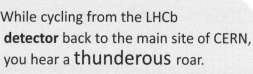

The hacker won't like that! Flip the corner or the other page.

While cycling from the LHCb **detector** back to the main site of CERN, you hear a **thunderous** roar.

You turn back to have a look.

"AAAAAAAAAHHHHHHH!" you shriek.

"Oh my goodness, it is a D-I-N-O-S-A-U-R!" you stare at it breathlessly.

No kidding! A theropod **dinosaur** is just a few metres away. It is a massive adult carnivorous beast with razor-sharp teeth and frightening eyes. Those jaws look heavy enough to crush and devour you in one snap. The claws at the end of its three-toed limbs seem ready to rake you. And if that wasn't worrying enough, it lashes its tail angrily while emitting loud and ghastly roars. Your legs move up a gear, or maybe two.

Science Byte

How to sound like a dinosaur?

Actually, we do not know how **dinosaurs** sounded like because they became extinct long ago. So you might be wondering, how are the noises of **dinosaurs** produced in films? The *Velociraptor* sounds come from tortoises, horses and geese. The iconic roar of the *Tyrannosaurus rex* is sometimes created by mixing elephant and **dog** sounds. Palaeontologists, however, think that the T-Rex might have sounded more like the modern-day emu: it did not even roar but emitted grunting and thumping sounds.

A very, very long time ago, this type of theropod used to live not far from Geneva, in the region that corresponds to today's Jura Mountains—the exact mountain range you see in front of you while cycling back to CERN. Did you know that these mountains give the name to **Jurassic**—a period dominated by **dinosaurs** between 200 and 145 million years ago?

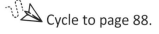

Cycle to page 88.

"When the **particle** beam is on, **protons** coming from both directions in the **LHC accelerator** meet here, colliding and transforming into a shower of other **particles**," explains Lesedi. "We need a huge instrument—like the one you see here—in order to detect them."

"What do you mean? How can **protons** become something else?" you ask.

"It's all about Einstein's formula: $E = mc^2$..." she says.

Science Byte

Einstein's famous equation, $E = mc^2$
· ·

E stands for energy, m for mass and c for... *celeritas* (which sounds like a magic spell, but it means "speed" in Latin, and in this case, the **speed of light**). c is a huge number and it is even multiplied by itself (c^2). Did you know that energy can become mass, and vice versa? With a lot of energy, you can make massive **particles**!

The **protons** start their journey with a certain mass and energy, but as they dash along the **LHC** ring, their energy increases. When they smash against each other inside the **detectors**, part of this energy can transform into new mass, in the form of new **particles**. The faster the **protons**, the higher the energy of their collision and the heavier the resulting **particles** can get.

Sun's problems   Quiz
· · · · · · · · · · · · · · · ·

The Sun burns **hydrogen**, the lightest gas in the Universe, and turns it into helium. Every second, it converts 600 million tonnes of **hydrogen** into 596 million tonnes of helium. Not bad… but what happens to the four million tonnes that go missing?

a) They completely transform into energy.

b) They disappear forever.

c) They get eaten by a black hole.

(Answer on page 157)

Nothing is created and nothing is destroyed, but everything is transformed.

Your tour of the LHCb **detector** is over, but the problems are just about to start.

Go to page 33.

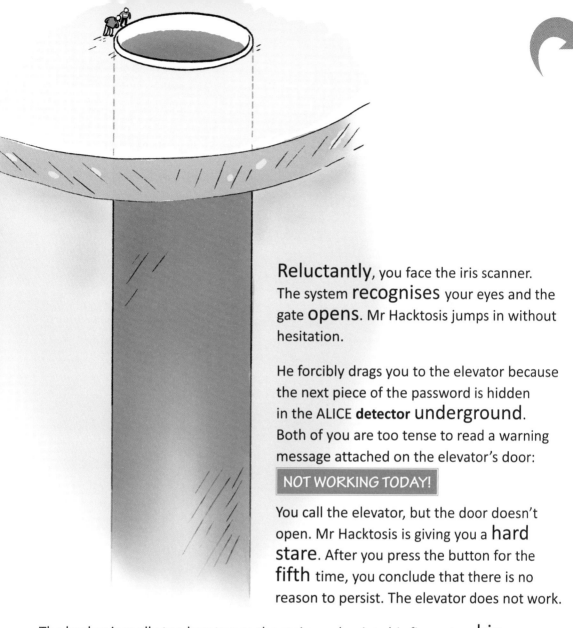

Reluctantly, you face the iris scanner. The system recognises your eyes and the gate opens. Mr Hacktosis jumps in without hesitation.

He forcibly drags you to the elevator because the next piece of the password is hidden in the ALICE **detector** underground. Both of you are too tense to read a warning message attached on the elevator's door:

NOT WORKING TODAY!

You call the elevator, but the door doesn't open. Mr Hacktosis is giving you a hard stare. After you press the button for the fifth time, you conclude that there is no reason to persist. The elevator does not work.

The hacker is really too lazy to use the stairs and points his finger to a big shaft, shouting: "Down!" Luckily, he chose a short word, so you manage to resist the stinky hurricane coming out of his mouth. By the way, this same shaft was used to lower down, one by one, all the components and pieces of equipment that make up the **detector**.

By any chance, did you choose two parachute vests as your tools on page 44?

- If you did, flip the top corner of this page.

- If not, flip the top corner of the opposite page.

Science Byte

How big were dinosaurs?

Have you ever measured the length of your feet and your legs? Try it out, then divide the length of your leg by the length of your foot. What do you get? For most people, the length of their leg is around 3–4.5 times the length of their foot. Believe it or not, the same is true for the terrible theropods! Hence, to calculate the length of the T-Rex leg, you just need to multiply the length of its footprint by four.

Theropods were bipeds; they walked on two legs. Other **dinosaurs**, like the sauropods, lumbered on four legs to support their titanic bulk. In the case of the sauropods, you need to draw a line between the two front feet, and another line to connect the two back feet. Then, find the middle point of both lines and measure the distance. This length corresponds to the length between the trunk and the hip of the **dinosaur**.

*If you want to take a break and prepare an edible **dinosaur** to wow your friends, go to the bonus material on page 161.*

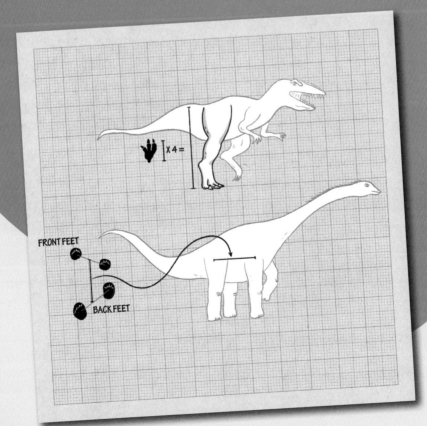

FRONT FEET

BACK FEET

X 4 =

Continue on the next page.

Stomping dinos

It is possible to differentiate major groups of **dinosaurs** by their footprints using clues such as the size and shape of a print, the geographic location and the age of the rocks. Quadruped (four-legged) **dinosaurs** usually had smaller front feet than back feet. Biped (two-legged) **dinosaurs** had scary-looking claws to grab their preys.

Theropods, such as *Tyrannosaurus* and *Velociraptor*, had long, slender toes and a V-shaped outline. Sauropods produced the largest **tracks** of all **dinosaurs**. They left wide and circular footprints, while their handprints were smaller.

Follow the **tracks** of these **dinosaurs** backwards to put their corresponding number in the right boxes. The answer to the equation will tell you where to go next.

(Solution on page 156)

$$\boxed{} + \boxed{} - \boxed{} + \boxed{} = \boxed{}$$

Spot the differences

Can you find all the differences between matter **particles** (**proton**, **electron** and **hydrogen**) and the corresponding mirror-image **antimatter particles**? Of course, Schrödy and his anticat companion at the bottom are just meddling; they aren't **particles** and do not count.

PROTON

ANTIPROTON

ELECTRON

ANTIELECTRON (POSITRON)

HYDROGEN

ANTIHYDROGEN

CAT

MEOW

WOEM

ANTICAT

(Solution on page 156)

The **dinosaur** is careening towards CERN's main site and is now in front of you. The **beast** seems angry, hungry and **ready to attack**. Everybody is running away in the opposite direction. You are the only one that follows the beast: this looks like an adventure you wouldn't want to miss. Not in a million years.

When the **dinosaur** reaches CERN, it heads towards a building called **antimatter** factory. While you are still panting and catching your breath, you get off the bike and try to think of your next move. How can you **stop** this **dinosaur**?

BEEEEEP BEEEEEP BEEEEEP

"Hi!" you answer the phone and it's your parents again.

"Hi! What are you doing, sweetheart? Are you running?" your mum asks.

"I'm heading to the **antimatter** factory," you reply.

"Really? Please ask an expert if they can really make an **antimatter** bomb, like in the science-fiction movies!" your dad suggests.

"Dad, you gave me a great idea! I will definitely ask! I need to go now. Bye!" you say while running inside the building.

Take the **antimatter** challenge on page 38.
When you are done, turn the page.

Science Byte

What's all this buzz about antimatter? (part 1)

. . . .

If **antimatter** comes in touch with matter, they both disappear. So if you can get enough **antimatter**, the **dinosaur** will disappear in a puff of energy.

Inside the **antimatter** factory, you stop to speak with someone hiding there.

"Did you see that huge **dinosaur** out there?" you ask a researcher at the **antimatter** factory.

"I sure did, it's pretty hard to miss," she replies. "That's why I am hiding here."

"Can you make an **antimatter** bomb, just a little one to scare the **dinosaur** away?" you ask, feeling hopeful.

"Sorry chap, I guess you've watched too many science-fiction movies," she explains. "It would take us millions of years to produce enough **antimatter** to make a bomb."

Curiously CERN

What's all this buzz about antimatter? (part 2)

. . . .

While a regular **atom** has positively **charged protons** and neutral **neutrons** in the **nucleus**, and negatively **charged electrons**, **antimatter** is just the opposite. **Antimatter** has negative anti**protons** in its **nucleus** and positive anti**electrons** (also called positrons) flying around it. Researchers at the **antimatter** factory are studying the properties of **antimatter** and producing anti**hydrogen atoms** made of anti**protons** and anti**electrons**.

Quiz

Where can you find antimatter?

. . . .

a) Only in outer space and physics laboratories

b) Only in physics laboratories

c) In bananas

(Answer on page 158)

Unfortunately, your first idea has failed. It is time to rack your brain and get creative.

Go to page 22.

Cheepy is just under the roof! Schrödy managed to push him **beyond** his limits. The little bird is shaking with fear of both the height and the presence of the cat.

It's quite **high** up there, and Schrödy is falling down. Will he land without getting hurt?

Your heart skips a beat to page 50.

This cake tastes great. You eat it slowly and carefully. Maybe this slice contains the *fève*, but the worst thing would be to swallow it. No sign of the *fève* after the first bite, nothing after the second bite, nothing after the third bite. Only a small piece is left.

"Never mind, I won't be the king of the day," you start to think.

Then, at the fourth bite, you feel something hard between your teeth and your tongue. "I got it! I got it!" you say, leaping with joy. You spit out a mini circular object. Everybody claps and says, "Congratulations!"

While admiring this strange *fève*, Loris tells you: "Today is your lucky day! And I have more good news for you. Since there is no particle beam running inside the **LHC** today and you are the king of the day, you are allowed to visit the LHCb **detector**!"

"Really?" you ask with a big smile.

"Yes! You can reach it by bike. There is one parked right there. To open the lock, just crack the code," says Loris.

"What code?" you ask.

"I shall give you a clue: remember the letters L-H-C-b. The rest is on the *fève*," Loris smiles and hands you a magnifying glass.

Deciphering a bike lock?

"Remember L-H-C-b, the rest is on the *fève*," you remind yourself Loris' words.

Using the magnifying glass, you discover that the *fève* is actually a mini cipher wheel with letters and numbers written on it. To decipher the code, find the number that corresponds to each letter of the word "LHCb". The resulting four-digit code will unlock the bike chain.

Go to the page corresponding to the last two digits of the code. If you get stuck, take a peek at the solution on page 157. If you are wondering where the LHCb **detector** is, have a look at the map on pages 2–3.

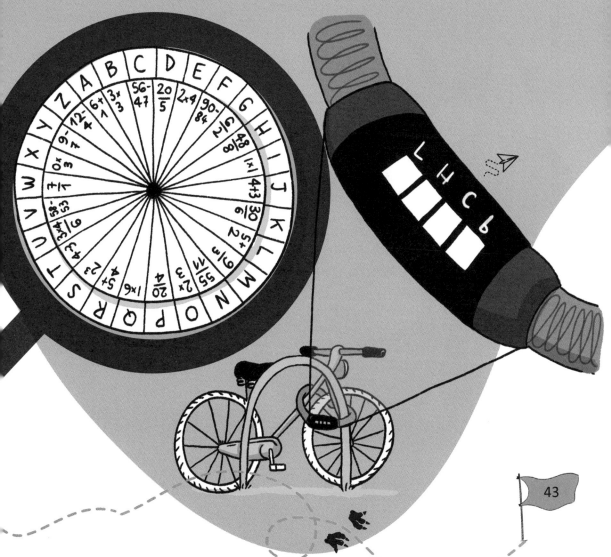

If you choose to be a CERN researcher...

All you need to do is get a password! That's your mission. All clear?

Are you asking **why?** Oh, there is no time for a long explanation at this stage.

Choose your helper

You are going to face a lot of **hurdles** and you won't be able to make it without a helper. Who could you possibly need? It is not an easy choice. Follow your **gut feeling** and choose one option:

○ One of the best operators of the CERN Control Centre (CCC)

○ Albert Einstein

○ A **dog**

PLEASE
don't choose the dog!

Choose your tools

You will also need to select two of these tools to make it through this whimsical adventure:

○ A torch

○ Two vests with parachute

○ Special contact lenses

○ A glass of water

○ A ruler

Tip: Put a tick next to your choices!

Who is Albert Einstein?

Albert, who sometimes stuck his tongue out, sticks out as one of the most famous physicists in history. Did you know that as a child, he disliked socks, loved playing with **magnets**, and was not very good at school? His headmaster even told him that nothing would ever come of him. Well, he must have been so embarrassed when Albert won the **Nobel Prize** in Physics in 1921.

Thanks to his theories about relativity and the **photoelectric effect**, we have lasers, automatic door openers and smartphones with the Global Positioning System (GPS)—a network of satellites and ground stations that tells you where you are.

After he died, his brain was removed and analysed to understand what made him a genius, but not much came out of these studies. You will read more about him in this book.

Life is like riding a bicycle. To keep your balance, you must keep moving.

Hopefully, now you have all you need.
Turn the page and **good luck!**

At first glance, it looks like **a real mess**. Filled with countless sheets of paper, books and journals, your office at CERN shows that you are **not the tidiest** person in the world. Handwritten notes **lie everywhere** on your desk, together with technical reports, a high pile of books and some mugs. Around the room are more books and storage boxes filled with wires, computer gizmos and logic games which have been salvaged over the years.

There is **hardly** any space left in your office. Finding something can be challenging, but that's just the way you like it.

Even the walls of your office are **covered** with posters of conferences, photos and mathematical equations. Some images are really intriguing. Have a closer look.

! ? ✓
Quiz
Did you spot a penguin? What's that?
. . . .

a) The symbol of another research institute

b) Just a penguin without any other meaning

c) The result of a bet among physicists

(Answer on page 150)

Quiz
What's this image with spirals and lines?

a) A photo of **particles** produced in a bubble chamber

b) Contemporary art

c) Scribbles that you drew when you were bored

(Answer on page 150)

You have just flown back from a long conference on the other side of the planet, and your colleagues will be back tomorrow. It's morning in Geneva but still night in California. Long flights and time differences always make you tired and **jet-lagged**, but you have to catch up with all the work and latest results of last week.

You start the day with hot chocolate, poured into your favourite mug, the one with the formula of the **Standard Model of particle physics** printed on it. You are about to savour the warm sweet drink when suddenly, you hear a racket coming from the corridor.

 Go to page 78.

You solve it without any problem: it's the letter **P**.

Mr Hacktosis, on the other hand, is still squinting his eyes, trying to follow the right wire. That gives you a brief advantage, and you seize the opportunity to **RUN away** from him!

Prof. Virtualli placed the next piece of the password somewhere along the **LHC tunnel** between the ALICE **detector** and the ATLAS **detector**.

Where do you go from here? You can use the map on pages 2–3, if you need, bearing in mind that you are **still** 100 metres underground.

Watching the arrow sign that points to ATLAS, you have a flash of genius: all you need is a glass of water!

By any chance, did you choose a **glass of water** as your tool on page 44?

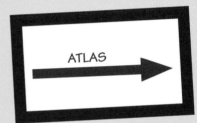

➤ If you did, go to page 77.

➤ If not, go to page 18.

Only a firefighter can help you. Flip the corner of the other page.

The man stops eating his chocolate and looks at you with disgust.

"I can understand **dogs** on public transport, but birds?!!?!" complains the man sternly.

"But..." you wish to explain.

"What's next?" interrupts the man. "What if it bites someone? What if it poops in the tram? What if it flies everywhere? Why don't you carry it inside a cage? Why don't you use a bird muzzle?" he insists.

"A bird muzzle for my Cheepy?" you are shocked.

What a headache! You try to explain that Cheepy is super well behaved and trained to relieve himself only at appropriate places. But there is no way to convince this man. You decide to just stand up and find another seat. Luckily, the place next to the girl is still available.

Go to page 94.

Did you know that falling cats have actually contributed to modern physics?

When dropped from upside down, cats are able to turn super fast, without any outside force, and land perfectly on their feet. In the late 1800s, some physicists thought that falling cats were defying the laws of physics. The mystery was solved only in 1969, and it turns out that cats do not break any physics laws.

When falling, the cat bends at the waist thanks to its ultra-flexible backbone. It forms a V shape and twists the front half of its body first.

Its front legs are pulled in, so its upper body rotates quickly: it's the same trick that figure skaters use to spin faster.

Then the cat flips its back part of the body, tucking its back legs under its body and extending its front legs.

No problem for Schrödy! He lands **uninjured!**

When it is about to land, all its legs are stretched out, so rotation stops.

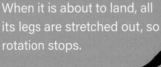

Without thinking, you climb onto the sheave of a **crane** to try to save Cheepy. This technical equipment, however, should not be meddled with, and an **alarm** goes off. You are losing balance... It is not looking good.

Did you choose a firefighter as your helper on page 11?

- If you did, flip the top corner of this page.

- If not, flip the top corner of the opposite page.

Great! Continue your adventure on page 24.

Unfortunately, Mr Hacktosis is much **faster** than you. He **gets hold** of the password hidden in the **LHC** tunnel between ALICE and ATLAS **before** you. That's too bad.

Go back to page 77 and choose another way to use the glass of water.

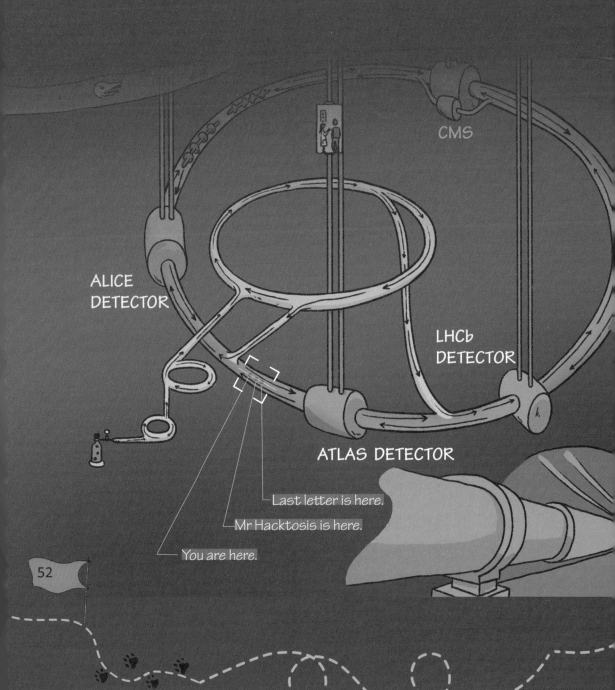

CMS

ALICE DETECTOR

LHCb DETECTOR

ATLAS DETECTOR

Last letter is here.

Mr Hacktosis is here.

You are here.

An animal trainer! Why not?

Nobody has ever **tamed** a **dinosaur**, but you can bet that Leonie—an animal trainer who has had several face-to-face encounters with **big predators**—will have some tricks up her sleeves.

Leonie says she wants to test an experimental method to calm the **dinosaur**: **hypnotise** it!

"To warm up, I need to practise on a smaller animal," she says, turning her eyes towards **Schrödy**. The cat doesn't even have the time to run away, and she plunges him into a deep hypnotic state.

"Great! It works!" says Leonie triumphantly. "Beast, it's now **your** turn! Here I come!"

Leonie approaches the roaring **dinosaur** confidently as the animal moves towards her. They are **dangerously** close to each other and you hope for the best.

It seems that she is making some progress. The **dinosaur** stops roaring and its movements become **jittery**. Then it freezes completely with its gaping jaws and a **malevolent** expression, like stuffed animals in natural history museums. Perplexed, Leonie looks at you and says: "Actually, I **haven't** done anything!"

WHAT?!?!

Turn the page with disbelief.

Why is the **dinosaur** frozen, you wonder. It is as if nothing has happened! Suddenly, everything is peaceful.

Confused by this ending? Choose another storyline to unravel the truth behind this mysterious ending.

Do you want to find out where the **dinosaur** came from?

Do you want to have a stroll around the town, explore CERN from an unexpected point of view and find out what Schrödy is up to?

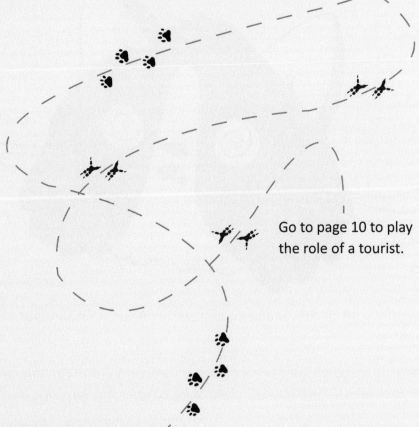

Go to page 10 to play the role of a tourist.

Go to page 44 to play the role of a CERN researcher.

Have you completed all the three stories?
Go to the epilogue on page 148.

It is lunch break and **nobody** is around to ask for help. There is not much you can do, so you grab the helmets, **dosimeters** and safety shoes, which are all **compulsory** for accessing the ALICE **detector**. Mr Hacktosis does not want you or anybody else to get the password because it would mean that his **nasty** "game" is over. At the same time, he needs you to help him **find** his way around and **enter places** with restricted access.

For example, this gate has a security system that works by scanning the **iris**, the coloured ring around the pupil of the eye. No two are exactly the same: irises are **unique**, like fingerprints. The iris scanner recognises people whose eyes have been registered in advance, so **only** those working at CERN can enter.

The hacker knows about it. "Scan **your eyes** and let me in!" he shouts.

You approach the iris scanner with a bit of hesitation.

Did you choose the **special contact lenses** as a tool on page 45?

→ If you did, go to page 105.

→ If not, go to page 35.

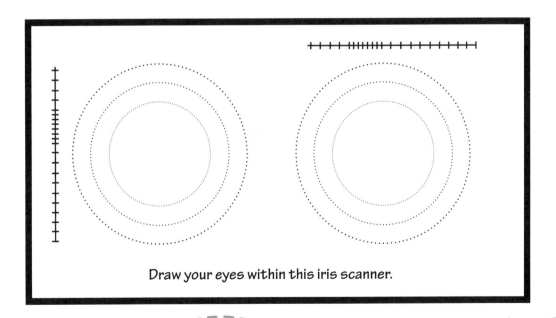

Draw your eyes within this iris scanner.

After this fantastic day, you thank Loris and decide to spend the evening in the **city centre** of Geneva.

BEEEeeEp BEEEeeEp BEEEeEp

That's your phone ringing. It's your parents calling. You pick up and say, "Hi!"

"Hi! How was your day?" ask your parents.

"It was **fantastic!**" you reply with a tonne of enthusiasm.

"Great! We just wanted to know if all's well with you," explain your parents.

"Yes, it's perfect. I am going to explore the city centre now," you say.

"Have fun and take care," say your parents, reassured.

After a 30-minute tram ride, you end up walking in a beautiful park, called *Parc des Bastions*. There, you find giant **chessboards** that anybody can play with. What a great idea! You play a game of chess with a **tourist**, but you lose. Never mind...

The next day, you are back at CERN with plenty of energy. It is Loris' **birthday** and everybody is celebrating at the CERN restaurant.

Some of the invitees have just finished their night shift. **Accelerators** and experiments need to be **monitored** 24 hours a day, seven days a week, so some researchers take turns to work **overnight** shifts.

It is peak hour and the restaurant is bustling with people of all ages and nationalities. The official languages spoken at CERN are **English** and **French**, but you can hear a lot of different languages. It is common for people who work at CERN to speak two or more languages.

"May I take a picture of your whole group?" you suggest.

While posing for the photo, everybody says "Cheeeese" as they would in their own countries. They choose some of the most hilarious expressions. That's a cacophony of sounds that makes you laugh out loud!

Say cheeeeese

Can you match the speech balloons to the people who say them?

If flags and languages aren't your thing, but you are curious to learn more, check out the answers on page 155.

Flash a big smile and turn the page.

SHUTDOWN: NO BEAM

While waiting for Loris' birthday cake, you notice some screens on the restaurant walls.

"The screens show the so-called **LHC Page 1** website, which is important for checking what's going on inside the **LHC accelerator**," explains Loris' colleague. "For example, '**SHUTDOWN: NO BEAM**' means that the **particles**, which travel in a beam, are not flying around CERN **accelerators** at the moment."

"Wow, researchers keep an eye on the performance of the **accelerators** even while they eat," you ponder.

Science Byte

What would happen if you stuck your head inside a particle accelerator while the particle beam is on?

You wouldn't want to try… Anatoli Bugorski is the only person known to have been exposed to a **particle accelerator's** beam. In 1978, while studying at the Institute of High Energy Physics in Russia, he leaned into the largest Soviet **particle accelerator**, the U-70 synchrotron, and a burst of high-energy **protons** travelled through his head. Since he was exposed to a lot of radiation, doctors feared the worst. Fortunately, he survived and went on studying even though he suffered occasional seizures, lost his hearing in one ear and was paralysed on one side of his face.

More recently, **protons** are used in some hospitals to treat cancer, but in this case, the beam accurately targets the tumour and the doses are around 300 times lower than the ones received by Anatoli.

Quiz

Accelerators for a myriad of uses

The **LHC** is a very special **accelerator**. The most common types of **particle accelerators** are not 27 kilometres long, but small **machines** used in companies and hospitals.

There are about 30,000 small **accelerators** worldwide. What are they used for?

a) Making electrical circuits

b) Treating cancer

c) Cleaning water

d) Boosting security

e) Making tastier chocolate and ice cream

f) All of the above, and more

(Answer on page 155)

Science Byte

Can accelerators satisfy your sweet tooth?

Yes, they can! Have you ever noticed the white coating that forms on the surface of chocolate? It is a defect caused by the melting properties of cocoa butter. A **particle accelerator**, called synchrotron, produces X-rays to help us see inside things, even inside chocolate. Some scientists and food manufacturers use this technology to improve their chocolate recipe and achieve the best mouthwatering chocolate.

"Hey, have you ever tasted the *Galette des rois*, the cake of the kings? Help yourself," encourages Loris.

This cake is not only a delicious French dessert, it is also a fun game. One slice of the cake contains a surprise called *fève* in French. Whoever finds it becomes the king of the day.

Is today your lucky day?
Which slice do you go for?

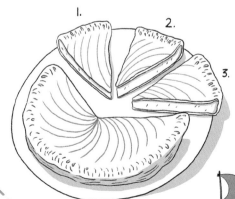

→ Slice 1: Go to page 62.

→ Slice 2: Go to page 42.

→ Slice 3: Go to page 142.

Did I hear bites? Do you mean that I eat 1,000,000,000,000,000 nuggets every year?

The **data centre** is the hub that **stores** the humongous amount of information generated at CERN: several PETABYTES per year, and counting!

What's a petabyte?

. . . .

Bytes (not bites, as Schrödy wants to hear) indicate the amount of data stored in computers and other electronic devices. Data could be videos, photos, messages, apps and so on.

Peta replaces the need to write a lot of zeros, **15 zeros** to be precise. For example, you use metres to measure short lengths, **kilometres** (which is equivalent to 1000 metres) to talk about longer distances, and you would need to travel about 40 **petametres** (40,000,000,000,000,000 metres) to reach the star Proxima Centauri, the closest star to us after the Sun. That's just mind-blowing, isn't it?

In the same way, the more data, videos, photos, etc. you want to store, the more bytes you need. Actually, to be even more precise, a petabyte is equal to 2 multiplied by itself for **50 times.** (2x2x2x2x2x2x2x2x2x2x.... Get the idea?) The result is **1,125,899,906,842,624.**

Try reading this number aloud. Do you feel your eyes bulging out just looking at it? It is much easier to say that a petabyte is approximately equal to 1, followed by 15 zeros.

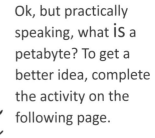

Ok, but practically speaking, what **is** a petabyte? To get a better idea, complete the activity on the following page.

The bytes labyrinth

Follow the lines to connect the funny little names tagged in front of "Byte" with the corresponding examples. What corresponds to a petabyte?

(Need help? Turn to page 151.)

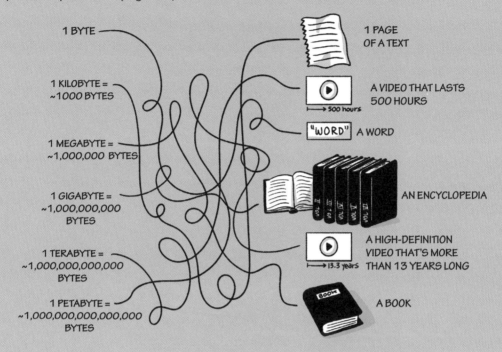

1 BYTE

1 KILOBYTE = ~1000 BYTES

1 MEGABYTE = ~1,000,000 BYTES

1 GIGABYTE = ~1,000,000,000 BYTES

1 TERABYTE = ~1,000,000,000,000 BYTES

1 PETABYTE = ~1,000,000,000,000,000 BYTES

1 PAGE OF A TEXT

A VIDEO THAT LASTS 500 HOURS
→ 500 hours

"WORD" A WORD

AN ENCYCLOPEDIA

A HIGH-DEFINITION VIDEO THAT'S MORE THAN 13 YEARS LONG
→ 13.3 years

A BOOK

Petabyte is not the largest you can go! We live in the era of BIG data. After petabytes, there are exabytes, zettabytes, yottabytes… For even bigger numbers, some people are thinking of using the word "brontobytes". "Bronto" means "thunder" in ancient Greek. Do you know another word that begins with "bronto"? The Brontosaurus (which means "thunder lizard")!

As soon as you enter the data centre, you discover that it is filled with small grey creatures, scurrying across the floor. A multitude of black eyes are looking at you, while their pointy noses sniff the air. You take a closer look and realise that you are facing a mice infestation!

Are you scared of mice?

→ AaahH… yes! Run to page 73.

→ If you are not or you are suspicious of these mice, go to page 140.

It would be nice to be the king of the day...

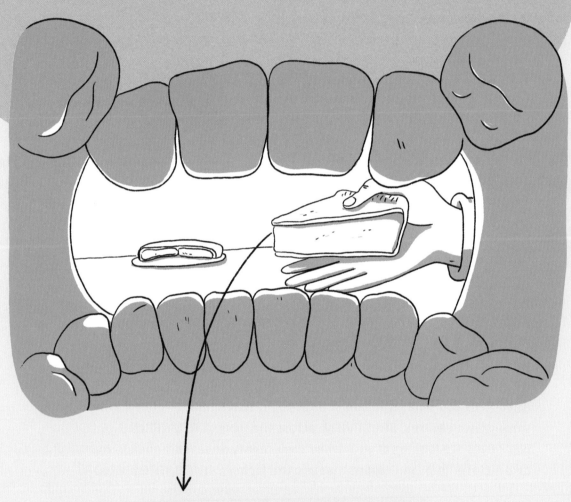

...but no luck today. You are left with some crumbs in your hands, but no *fève*. Choose another slice on page 59 and try your luck again.

"Oh! It is absolutely ginormous!" you exclaim, peering over the blue railing that separates you from the **biggest** and **most complex** man-made work you have ever seen. You need to turn your head up and down, left and right several times to scan this impressive **behemoth**.

You feel as if you are in the set of a **science-fiction** movie: a colourful composition of wires, cables, pipes and shining surfaces form what looks like a gigantic and high-tech **flower**. With a bit of fantasy, you can think of it as a **humongous** daisy.

Marta points her finger to the **centre** of the "flower" to show you the place where the **protons** enter in the **detector** when it is in operation. The "petals" are used to detect some **particles**, called **muons**, that come out of the **proton-proton** collision.

Curiously CERN

ATLAS: the largest detector

The ATLAS (<u>A</u> <u>T</u>oroidal **LHC** <u>A</u>pparatu<u>S</u>) **detector** is the largest **detector** ever built. It is longer than 2 train carriages (46 metres), taller than 5 giraffes standing one on top of another (25 metres) and as heavy as 1400 African elephants (7000 tonnes). It took over 10 years to construct it.

Turn the page to explore ATLAS inside out.

ATLAS

VROOM
VROOM

VROOM
VROOM

ATLAS

64

A bunch of **protons** coming from the left and another bunch of **protons** coming from the right collide in the middle of ATLAS and produce a shower of **particles.**

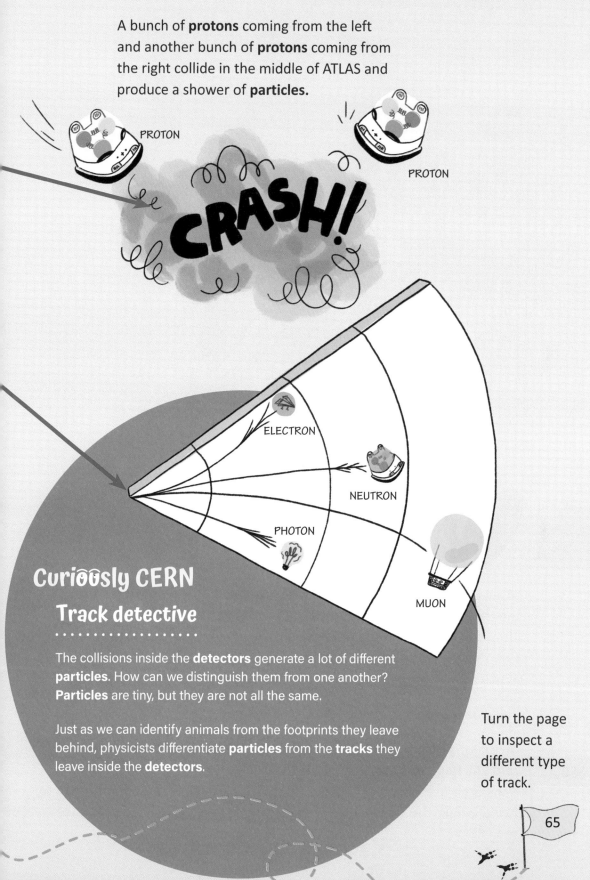

PROTON

PROTON

CRASH!

ELECTRON

NEUTRON

PHOTON

MUON

Curiously CERN
Track detective

The collisions inside the **detectors** generate a lot of different **particles**. How can we distinguish them from one another? **Particles** are tiny, but they are not all the same.

Just as we can identify animals from the footprints they leave behind, physicists differentiate **particles** from the **tracks** they leave inside the **detectors**.

Turn the page to inspect a different type of track.

Quiz

Which is the right track?

Can you recognise the footprints of the *Triceratops*?

(Answer on page 154)

Marta, your CERN guide, explains that ATLAS and CMS researchers proved the **existence** of a new **particle** called **Higgs boson** in 2012. A year after, two physicists who had predicted the existence of this **particle** were awarded the **Nobel Prize** in Physics, and the scientists working on the ATLAS and CMS experiments were mentioned too.

"How does the **Higgs boson** look like?" you ask.

"Actually, we can't take a picture of this **particle** directly. No **detector** can! The **Higgs boson**'s existence is fleeting: the instant it appears, it transforms immediately," explains Marta. "For example, it can transform into two **photons**, the same **particles** that make up light."

Catching the Higgs boson

The **Higgs boson** is important to understand why some **particles** have mass. If **particles** had no mass, they would whizz around the Universe at the **speed of light**. Hence, without **Higgs boson**, there wouldn't be any **atoms**, any **molecules**, and… needless to say, humans would not even exist!

Particle Sudoku

Take a little break to play this **Particle** Sudoku. Fill the empty boxes with the images of **particles** such that there is only one of each type of **particle** in any column, row or mini-grid.

The **particles** featured here are: **photons, electrons, Higgs bosons, muons, protons** and the hypothetical **dark matter particles**. You can either draw them or cut out the images provided on the last page of the book to complete the puzzle.

Note: **Particles** don't look like this for real… but it's nice to add a bit of creativity and colour.

PROTON   MUON

ELECTRON   PHOTON

DARK MATTER   HIGGS BOSON

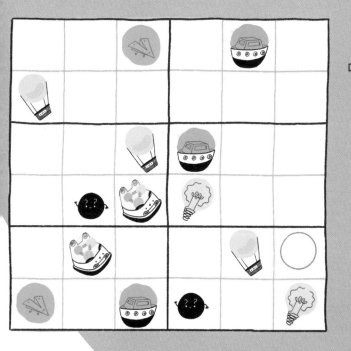

Which **particle** goes inside the red circle?

a) **Higgs boson**

b) **Photon**

c) **Proton**

(If you get really stuck, take a peek at the solution on page 154.)

When you are done with the *sudoku*, turn the page.

As you are leaving ATLAS, you see a cat running **wildly** towards Cheepy. It is the **fastest** cat you have ever seen, dashing as if there are skates under its feet!

"Schrödy! Leave the poor bird alone!" shouts Marta. But the feline pays minimal attention; his animal **instinct** rules.

The cat's name is inspired by a well-known physicist, called **Erwin Schrödinger** (1887–1961). He is famous for a thought experiment that involves a cat: it's an experiment that you can think of, but you cannot really perform practically.

The paradox of the zombie cat

Erwin Schrödinger is best known for a paradox—that is an absurd thought —about a zombie cat. Flex your brain because this is the weirdest thing you will hear today, guaranteed.

This paradox says that if a cat and a radioactive substance are placed in a box for an hour, there is a 50% chance that the radioactive substance will kill the cat. But if you keep the box closed, you do not know what happens to the animal. According to common sense, the cat inside the box is EITHER alive OR dead. However, you could also think that the feline could be in a sort of zombie state: alive AND dead at once. And only by looking inside the box, you force the cat to be either alive or dead.

Erwin himself considered this paradox crazy and ridiculous. Everybody knows that cats cannot be dead and alive at the same time. The paradox shows that big objects, such as animals, behave differently from microscopic **particles**. Very strange things happen in the **particles'** world; common sense and **quantum physics** don't always match… For example, it is normal for **particles** to exist in two places at the same time and to have a double nature. Only when you observe and measure **particles** do they take a definite position.

Prof. Schrödinger became famous thanks to cats, so I expect a feast with a mouth-watering selection of food made with fat mice, fresh fish and delicious birds.

What's this monkey business? Seriously, what did Prof. Schrödinger have against cats?

Why didn't he choose a flea-bitten dog for his mental experiments? That's paradoxical!

Why choose a cat for this silly paradox?

Turn the page.

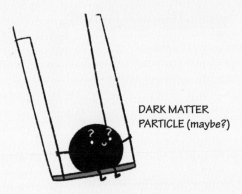

DARK MATTER
PARTICLE (maybe?)

Marta looks at you and explains: "Sorry, we tried to tame this cat, but he is **incorrigible**. He was a stray cat... We kind of adopted him."

Cheepy is escaping as fast as he possibly can, but Schrödy is always behind.

"Oh, maybe they are just playing," you try to **defuse** the situation, hoping that your pet is well.

Marta concludes the tour with some final remarks about the **unsolved mysteries** of physics and the whole group applauds her. It was even more fascinating than what you'd expected. Your mind is now **bubbling** with ideas about **particles**, **dark matter** and **antimatter**.

It's when you remove the safety helmet and adjust your hat that the thought of Cheepy comes back. You turn around, but you don't see any sign of your friend. The cat has **disappeared** as well.

"Cheepy, where have you gone?" you call out to him.

You do not want to abandon your pet, but how are you going to find Cheepy in this unfamiliar place? Read on to find out.

Great choice! Go to page 144.

You enter the first building you see just down the road. The large letters on the building spell: IdeaSquare.

Cheepy knows that he should not enter any building, but he might have made a mistake while **running away** from Schrödy.

You have a look around. This place has a lot of small meeting rooms but **no sign** of the two animals. If Cheepy is not here, then he must have flown farther away.

CERN is a rather big place. How are you going to get around? Coincidentally, you spot an unusual means of transport just around the corner. A message reads: Use in emergency.

"Oh, I'm so lucky! Someone thought to park a **double-decker bus** here for me!" you exclaim.

You decide to drive to CERN's **tallest** building. Cheepy might be visible from there.

You go straight to the **top floor** where there is a terrace just below the roof. Luckily, someone left the door open, so you have easy access to the terrace. From up here, you have a better view of the campus.

The tool you selected on page 11 might be useful now.

→ If you chose the bag of groceries, go to page 76.

→ If you chose a bag of bird seeds, go to page 92.

→ If you chose the binoculars, go to page 31.

There is no time to waste and only **one way** to solve this problem: find the password to unlock Prof. Virtualli's laptop and stop a potential **disaster** from happening.

You rush to the CCC, which stands for CERN Control Centre. It is located in Prévessin village, in France, less than 10 minutes' drive from CERN's main site.

Did you choose the **CCC operator** as your helper on page 44?

- If you did, flip the top corner of this page.

- If not, flip the top corner of the opposite page.

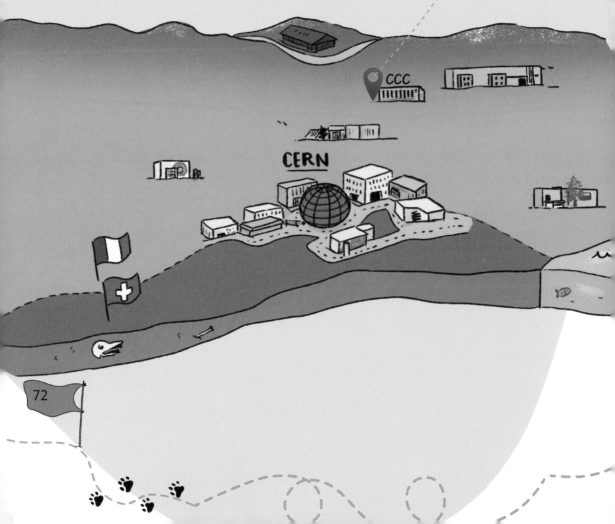

Squeaking mice are your **worst nightmare** by far. You run away as **fast** as you can.

Complete and colour in the drawing of yourself running away with a horrified expression as you escape from the mice.

I am scared of loud appliances, like vacuum cleaners and blenders, popping balloons, vet doctors, cucumbers, but above all, DOGS!!!

Your adventure ends here, but that's a real pity. The truth is that these are not real mice. Go to page 140 to find out where they come from by attempting to complete the mission.

Sorry, the **dog** and Einstein can't help you, only the CCC operator can. Flip the corner of the other page.

Being magnetic is not enough... the **LHC magnets** have other SUPER-duper properties: they work thanks to SUPERconductivity at SUPER cold temperatures. That's SUPERlative!

I am a SUPER cat!

Science Byte

SSSSSUPER science

.... Have you felt that some of your electrical appliances, like your vacuum cleaner, become warmer when they are used for a long time? This is due to resistance, which means that the device does not use the entire **current** and loses some of it as heat. Superconducting materials are way better! They are among the most exciting materials discovered because they do not have resistance!

The problem, however, is that they are superconducting only at incredibly low temperatures; this property disappears when you warm them up a bit. By the way, if you manage to discover superconductors that work at reasonable temperatures (such that we can use them in everyday objects), you will become famous and revolutionise how energy is used around the world!

SUPERCONDUCTING MATERIAL

Curiously CERN

The biggest "SUPER freezer" in the world

Your fridge keeps milk at roughly 0–5°C (32–41°F) and your freezer cools your ice-cream down to a teeth-chattering –20°C (–4°F). However, these temperatures are nothing compared to the coldness required to run the **LHC magnets**: –271°C (–456°F)! That is colder than outer space. Hence, you can say that the **LHC** is also the biggest "SUPER freezer" in the world.

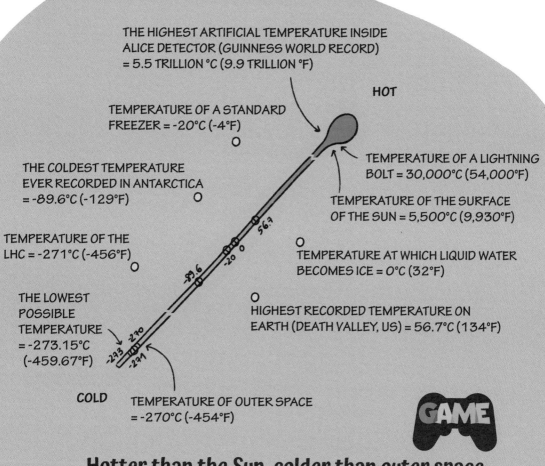

THE HIGHEST ARTIFICIAL TEMPERATURE INSIDE ALICE DETECTOR (GUINNESS WORLD RECORD) = 5.5 TRILLION °C (9.9 TRILLION °F)

HOT

TEMPERATURE OF A STANDARD FREEZER = -20°C (-4°F)

TEMPERATURE OF A LIGHTNING BOLT = 30,000°C (54,000°F)

THE COLDEST TEMPERATURE EVER RECORDED IN ANTARCTICA = -89.6°C (-129°F)

TEMPERATURE OF THE SURFACE OF THE SUN = 5,500°C (9,930°F)

TEMPERATURE OF THE LHC = -271°C (-456°F)

TEMPERATURE AT WHICH LIQUID WATER BECOMES ICE = 0°C (32°F)

THE LOWEST POSSIBLE TEMPERATURE = -273.15°C (-459.67°F)

HIGHEST RECORDED TEMPERATURE ON EARTH (DEATH VALLEY, US) = 56.7°C (134°F)

COLD

TEMPERATURE OF OUTER SPACE = -270°C (-454°F)

Hotter than the Sun, colder than outer space

Draw straight lines to connect the tiny yellow circles of the descriptions to the correct temperature on the thermometer. The lines will form a three-digit number: that's the number of the page you need to go next.

(Need help? Turn to page 152.)

Cheepy should be able to see you here, so you decide to find a way to **catch** his attention.

"If I cannot see Cheepy, at least Cheepy will see me," you reckon. But how? What about creating a **volcanic** eruption?

It is such a **coincidence** that you have all the materials you need in your shopping bag.

Quiz

Which items would you use to make a red eruption that looks like volcanic lava?

· ·

Circle them. (Hint: You need 5 items.)

(Check if you've picked out the correct items on page 154.)

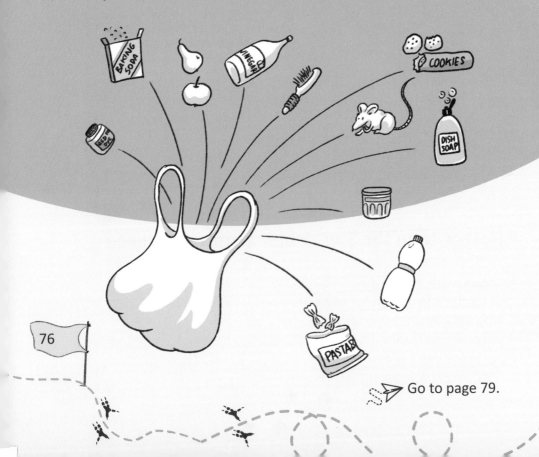

Go to page 79.

Can a **glass of water** help you? What happens if you put it in front of the arrow sign?

The direction of the arrow will flip. Go to page 25.

Nothing. You prefer to drink it up because it is going to be a long run to ATLAS. Go to page 52.

The arrow will look smaller, which is pointless. It is better to splash it on the face of the hacker. Continue reading here below.

Mr Hacktosis dodges the **splash** of water easily, and only a few drops reach him. Absolutely **furious**, he runs towards the ATLAS **detector**, and you don't have any hope of getting the remaining letter of the password **before** him. Do not despair; you can consider another use of the glass of water. Go back to the top of this page and choose either the first or second option.

As soon as you open the door of your office, a crowd of students passes in front of you, shouting: "**DINOSAURS' TEETH ARE LIKE KNIVES. RUN FOR YOUR LIVES!**" Then a bird whizzes in the opposite direction, chased by guess who? Schrödy. He loves chasing all sorts of preys around the campus.

"What's going on today? Is everybody going crazy?" you mumble. "Have students nothing better to do? And since when do we allow all these animals indoors? This is no longer a laboratory, it is a jungle!"

You return to your desk and try to concentrate. You need to access some data stored in the laptop of **Professor Virtualli**, a colleague of yours who recently passed away. You miss all the thoughtful discussions and long hours spent together with him. Handling his computer always makes you emotional and brings back a lot of beautiful memories. Wiping tears from your eyes, you notice that something unusual is going on. The computer is not responding; you are unable to click on anything. After a few seconds of shock, a message blinks on the screen, saying:

SECURITY WARNING!

SUSPECTED ATTACK BY A HACKER!

ENTER PASSWORD TO CONTINUE:

Hackers break into another person's computer, often because they want to steal information. This is really bad. 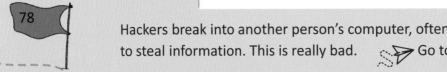 Go to page 139.

You fill the bottle with warm water, then add six drops of dish soap, one drop of red food colouring, and two tablespoons of baking soda.

"Here comes my favourite part of the experiment!" You slowly pour vinegar into the bottle, and... **"It's eruption time!"** you shout.

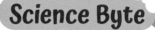

Science Byte

Eruption time
. . . .

A chemical reaction between the baking soda and vinegar produces carbon dioxide bubbles. The eruption happens because pressure builds up inside the bottle until the mixture overflows. The soap makes the "lava" foamy.

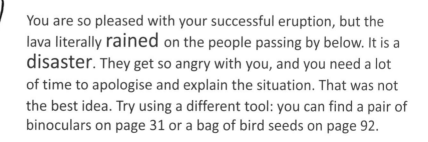

You are so pleased with your successful eruption, but the lava literally **rained** on the people passing by below. It is a **disaster**. They get so angry with you, and you need a lot of time to apologise and explain the situation. That was not the best idea. Try using a different tool: you can find a pair of binoculars on page 31 or a bag of bird seeds on page 92.

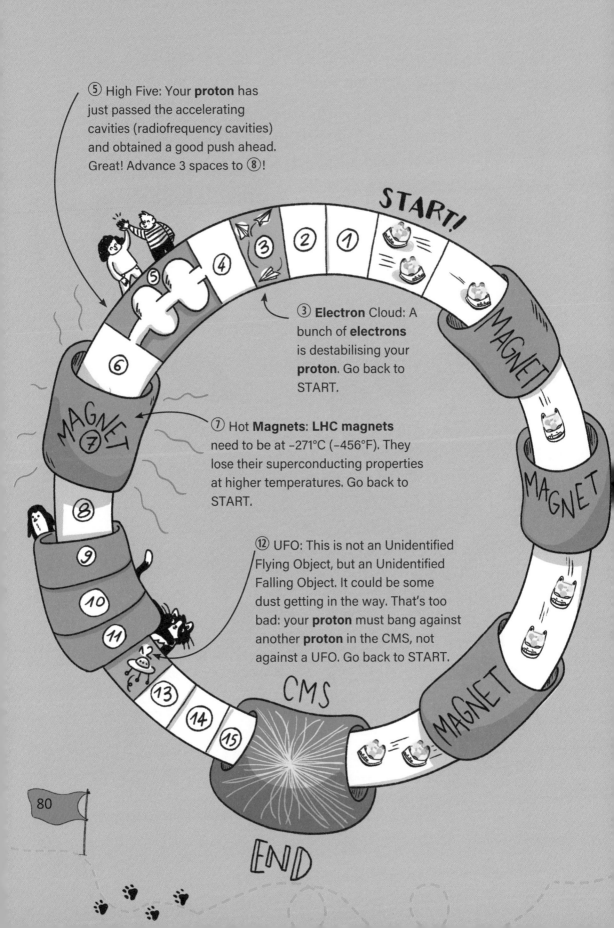

⑤ High Five: Your **proton** has just passed the accelerating cavities (radiofrequency cavities) and obtained a good push ahead. Great! Advance 3 spaces to ⑧!

START!

③ **Electron** Cloud: A bunch of **electrons** is destabilising your **proton**. Go back to START.

⑦ Hot **Magnets**: LHC magnets need to be at −271°C (−456°F). They lose their superconducting properties at higher temperatures. Go back to START.

⑫ UFO: This is not an Unidentified Flying Object, but an Unidentified Falling Object. It could be some dust getting in the way. That's too bad: your **proton** must bang against another **proton** in the CMS, not against a UFO. Go back to START.

CMS

END

The collision challenge

Now that you are safe, you can play this special board game.

Your piece is a **proton**, eager to smash inside the CMS **detector**. It's going to be a lucky collision that will generate a **Higgs boson**! You can feel it!

You goal is to move your **proton** anticlockwise from the START to the collision point (END).

Cut out your proton from the last page of the book.

Flip a coin.

- If you get heads, your **proton** moves closer by 1 space.

- If you get tails, it moves closer by 2 spaces.

Challenge: Can your **proton** reach the CMS **detector** with fewer than 11 coin tosses? Alternatively, race a friend to see whose **proton** reaches first.

To continue the adventure, go to page 23.

Now Marta proceeds to accompany you and the rest of the group to CERN's first **accelerator**—the synchrocyclotron. Wow, it sounds like a tongue twister, doesn't it? This machine is truly a gem in the history of CERN.

The synchrocyclotron was built in 1957 and fits inside a building. It is so small compared to the **LHC**, which is 27 kilometres in circumference. It is not used anymore, but it is still quite impressive. Inside this machine, **charged particles** were going around and around in a circular path.

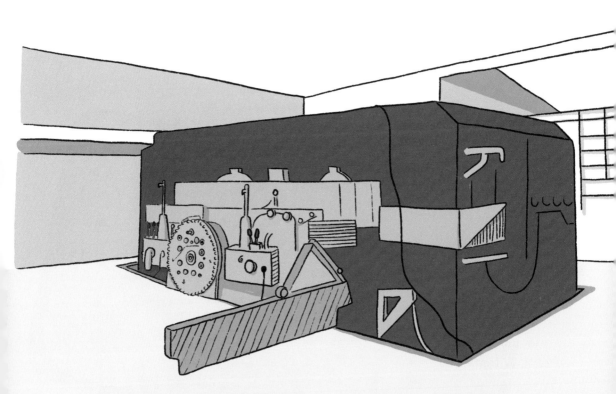

"And as the final highlight of the tour, I will take you to the ATLAS **detector**. It is possible to view it today because there are no **particles** running inside the **LHC accelerator**," continues Marta.

 Are you ready to explore the concrete cavern of ATLAS almost 100 metres

beneath the Earth's surface?

Go to page 63.

Find the intruders
· ·

The ability to focus and attention to detail are valuable skills for a researcher-to-be. Here is a game to test your acute visual skills. Find three intruders in this figure.

(Solution on page 158)

After the talk, the tour with Loris continues, and you keep your eyes wide open to explore everything that surrounds you.

You find out that the **majority** of the people working at CERN are not physicists but engineers and technicians. Loris also introduces you to some computer scientists engrossed in their work. It is impressive to see the sheer number of people from **all over the world** gathered at CERN. Within a year, more than **10,000** people come to CERN for work. Some are involved in **big** experiments, others in small ones. There are also those who take care of the **Large Hadron Collider (LHC)**, the **biggest** and **most powerful** **particle accelerator** on the planet.

In your mind, researchers wear white lab coats and have wild hair flying everywhere. You are surprised to see that this is not the case: nobody wears lab coats here at CERN, and most people have a neat haircut.

Turn the page.

You buy a **sweater** with a printed drawing of **particle** collisions and pose for a photo in front of a blue tube. This is a **magnet**, like the blue **magnets** of the **LHC accelerator**. You promised your friends back home to take a lot of cool pictures, and this is one of the most popular photo spots at CERN. Schrödy doesn't want to admit it, but he likes to be featured in photos too.

Doodle a cheerful expression on your face and complete the drawing with your favourite colours and hairstyle.

If you are wondering what's inside the blue LHC magnet, have a look at the bonus material on page 159. A sweet surprise awaits you.

Once you are done, go to page 56.

Now the question is: **Where** is the password hidden?

Luckily, you see an engineer approaching.

"Don't even **think** about reporting me, otherwise I..." says the hacker. This time his mouth is open for far too long and the effect is **devastating**.

"Fine, fine, fine!" you want him to cut it short, so he shuts up.

"**Hi!** I have never seen you around," says the engineer. "Are you both **new** ALICE physicists?"

"No," you answer, but Mr Hacktosis gives you an aggressive tug.

"Oh **yes**, yes," you correct yourself quickly.

"Great! Welcome and nice to meet you! Don't hesitate to ask me **any** questions!" the engineer offers kindly.

"Actually, we are looking for a letter, you know..." you say, trying not to sound too **awkward**.

"Ah!" exclaims the engineer, a bit surprised. "**Rumours** spread very fast in this place. Someone said to someone who said to someone that someone hid a letter in this messy **tangle** of wires. But it's **just** a rumour," shrugs the engineer, without showing much interest. "Sorry, but I just remembered that I have a meeting. I need to go. See you around!"

Messy wires

Follow the arrow. The shape of the wire will reveal a letter. Try to find the letter quickly, before the hacker does! Then run as fast as you can to page 48.

(Solution on page 153)

Curiously CERN

The LHCb **detector** was built to study **particles** containing b-**quarks**, the so-called beauty **quarks**. This is indicated by the letter "b" in its name, LHCb, or Large Hadron Collider beauty experiment. It is 21 metres long (like a train carriage), 10 metres tall (like two giraffes, one miraculously standing on the head of the other) and weighs 5600 tonnes (approximately 1120 African elephants).

In this **detector**, the physicists found traces of exotic **particles**. When you think of something exotic, your mind probably wanders to some tropical beaches or rainforests. But this isn't that sort of exotic… These short-lived **particles** are exotic because they are made of four or five **quarks**! In our Universe, **quarks** and anti**quarks** love staying together in groups of two or three, not more. For example, nuclei of ordinary matter are made of **protons** and **neutrons**, which have three **quarks** each (see the *Matryoshka* doll on pages 6–7). These exotic **particles** have instead more than three **quarks**. It is therefore exhilarating to know that for just a fraction of a second, the **LHC** is able to recreate **particles** that do not exist anymore but were found a looong time ago—at the beginning of the Universe.

CLICK

Lesedi, Loris' colleague, is waiting for you at the entrance of the LHCb building. While walking to the elevator, she hands you a safety helmet and is happy to explain to you everything about the LHCb **detector**.

The elevator is very quick, and without even realising, you find yourself in a **huge cavern** 100 metres underground.

"Whoa! I have never seen anything like this!" you exclaim excitedly, **amazed** by the sight of the LHCb **detector**. "How does it work?"

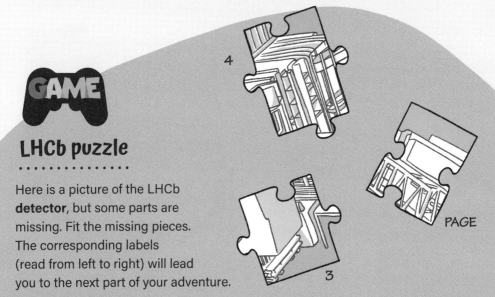

GAME

LHCb puzzle
· · · · · · · · · · · · · ·

Here is a picture of the LHCb **detector**, but some parts are missing. Fit the missing pieces. The corresponding labels (read from left to right) will lead you to the next part of your adventure.

GO TO _____ __ __.

(Solution on page 157)

GAME

The hidden meaning of dino words

Jurassic comes from Jura, but a lot of scientific words come from ancient Greek or Latin. Can you guess the meaning behind each **dinosaur** name? The description of each **dinosaur** contains some clues that will help you match each underlined part of the name to its meaning:

Dino _saur_
A group of reptiles that lived during the Mesozoic era, around 225 to 65 million years ago.

_Brachio_saurus
Like giraffes, this herbivorous dinosaur used its height to reach vegetation in trees. Its forelimbs were longer than its hindlimbs.

Veloci _raptor_
An agile meat-eater. It was only recently that palaeontologists discovered it had feathers. However, its wings were too short to fly.

lizard

arm

king

terrible

double

speedy

feather or wing

robber

horn

three

tyrant

beam

_Tyranno_saurus _rex_
The boss of the Cretaceous period needs no introduction.

Diplo _docus_
It had double-beamed chevron bones located in the underside of the tail, which were considered unique.

_Ptero_dactylus antiquus
It was technically not a dinosaur. It had a birdlike beak and massive wings. It could fly as well as walk on the ground.

Tri _cera_tops
This distinguished beast is known for having a bony crest on the neck, a long horn over each eye and a shorter horn on the nose. These were good weapons for fighting.

88

(Answers on page 157)

Science Byte

Jura, Jurassic and the longest sauropod trackway

Although it's hard to believe, the Jura Mountains visible from CERN were once a vast tropical beach where **dinosaurs** were roaming and frolicking. Back then, this region was bathed by a warm and shallow sea, dotted with small islands.

The longest sauropod trackway in the world was discovered about 50 kilometres from CERN. The site is called Dinoplagne®—from the name of the nearby village, Plagne. The palaeontologists (**dinosaur** experts) have named this **track**: *Brontopodus plagnensis*, which translates as "thunderfoot of Plagne". The 155-metre-long **track** consists of 111 footprints. A plant-eating, long-necked **dinosaur** that was 35 metres in length and 40 tonnes in weight left them almost 150 million years ago. According to the shape of the footprints, it was walking at a speed of 4 kilometres per hour, and it had big circular feet: 94 by 103 centimetres.

Not far from the long-necked **dinosaur** walked a bipedal three-toed theropod. This carnivore was smaller than the T-Rex but still quite impressive: 3 metres high and 9 metres long.

How are **dinosaur tracks** preserved for millions of years? Unlike **dinosaur** skeletons, which needed to be covered soon after the **dinosaur** died, their **tracks** needed to be baked hard by the Sun.

Continue to learn cool facts about **dinosaurs** on page 36.

The CCC always makes an impression on you with all its computers and screens showing **multicoloured** lines, tables, graphs and maps. CCC operators use this information to judge how well the **particles** are running inside CERN **accelerators**.

Every detail is **meticulously** planned, checked and double-checked. How **fascinating!**

What are all these screens for?

Several computer stations are used to monitor if everything is working smoothly inside CERN **accelerators**. **Protons** flying clockwise and anticlockwise inside the **LHC accelerator** need to smash against each other in the **detectors**. This is no trivial task, because **particles** are very, very small and the **LHC** is very, very long! It is like taking aim and firing two green peas from a great distance to make them meet halfway: it is almost impossible unless you align their flying paths super carefully.

Have you noticed some bottles of champagne around the walls? These are gifts from researchers working at the four big **detectors** (ALICE, ATLAS, CMS and LHCb) and other experiments. It is their way of saying "Thank you" to the CCC operators for the successful results, which were made possible because of the good **particle** alignment.

This bottle was sent by your research team. Write or doodle a thank-you message on the label.

When you are done, go to page 106.

Your bag of bird seeds attracts a lot of **local birds**.

"I'm so glad that you have come in such great numbers. My feathered friend is **missing**. His name is Cheepy. He is a lovely cockatiel. Here is his picture," you explain, showing a photo of Cheepy on your phone.

"Please can you look for him, and spread the news to your **friends**," you say.

"*Cheep-cheep*," chirp the birds in excitement while filling their bellies.

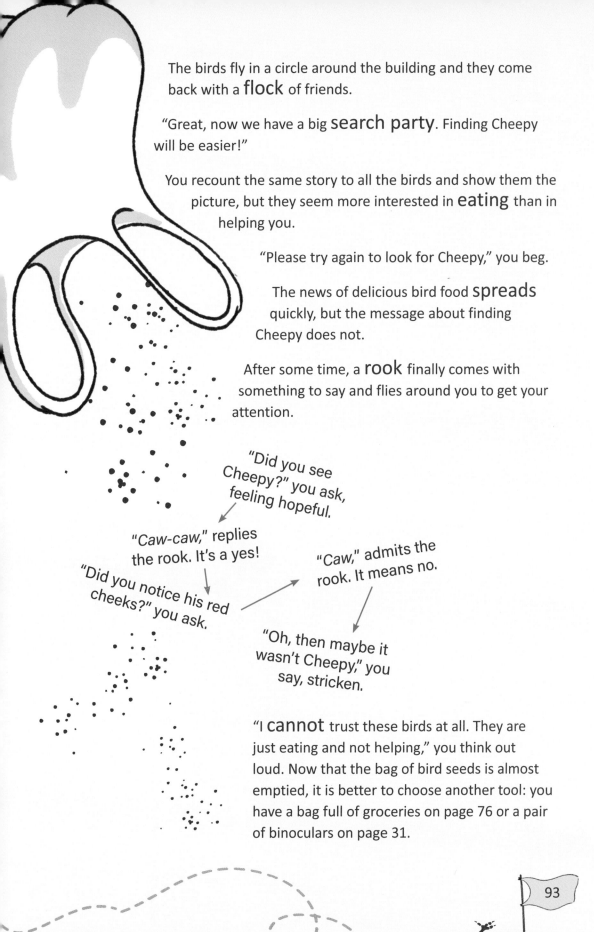

The birds fly in a circle around the building and they come back with a **flock** of friends.

"Great, now we have a big **search party**. Finding Cheepy will be easier!"

You recount the same story to all the birds and show them the picture, but they seem more interested in **eating** than in helping you.

"Please try again to look for Cheepy," you beg.

The news of delicious bird food **spreads** quickly, but the message about finding Cheepy does not.

After some time, a **rook** finally comes with something to say and flies around you to get your attention.

"Did you see Cheepy?" you ask, feeling hopeful.

"Caw-caw," replies the rook. It's a yes!

"Did you notice his red cheeks?" you ask.

"Caw," admits the rook. It means no.

"Oh, then maybe it wasn't Cheepy," you say, stricken.

"I **cannot** trust these birds at all. They are just eating and not helping," you think out loud. Now that the bag of bird seeds is almost emptied, it is better to choose another tool: you have a bag full of groceries on page 76 or a pair of binoculars on page 31.

The girl is typing **frenetically**, absorbed in her laptop. Then all of a sudden, she closes her laptop and shakes her head with a disappointed face. You cannot help but notice a blue CERN sticker on the cover of her laptop. Great! She must be working at CERN, you think.

"Hi! My name is .... [insert your name]. I am visiting CERN today. Are you heading there as well?" you ask politely.

"Hi, my name is **Marta**. Yes, I work at CERN, and I'm also a CERN **guide**. I accompany visitors around CERN and explain to them how the experiments work. I've just read that my friend who was booked for today's group visit is not going to make it. Would you like to **replace** him?" she proposes.

"Really? Of course! Thank you so much!" you say with a **smile** that reaches all the way to your eyes.

"Only one thing: your lovely bird is **not allowed** to enter the buildings. But it can fly anywhere outdoors," Marta points out.

"I understand," you say half-heartedly. "My little friend will **enjoy** some fresh air. Won't you, Cheepy?"

Cheepy does not look very convinced, but he accepts the rule anyway.

CANISTER OF
HYDROGEN

The tram stops at CERN. You follow Marta while Cheepy zigzags lazily around the poles displaying the flags of the countries that promote and fund CERN research.

A group of people is waiting at the reception, and Marta is happy to see them. "Welcome to CERN!" she greets. "I am your guide for today. Please follow me to discover more about the secrets of the Universe."

Marta starts her tour by explaining where the **particles** that run inside the **LHC** come from: "Here at CERN, we have some of the most complex technologies on Earth, but everything starts from a plain canister of **hydrogen**."

Hydrogen is a very simple atom: it has only one **electron** and one **proton**.

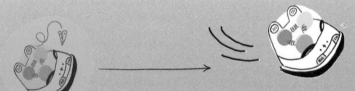

The **electrons** are removed from the **hydrogen atoms**, and the **protons** continue their journey.

"These **protons** fly faster and faster until they reach the huge **LHC** ring, the biggest **accelerator** on Earth. At that stage, they are travelling almost at the **speed of light**," explains Marta with contagious excitement.

"Then we make them smash together," she adds, describing the **particle** collision as if it was the most normal thing on Earth.

Turn the page.

Track and smash

This is a schematic representation of CERN **accelerators'** system. Follow the path of four **protons** from the canister of **hydrogen** to the collision points where they crash. Two **protons** collide inside the CMS **detector** and the other two inside the LHCb **detector**. Which lines show the original paths of the two **protons** that crash inside the CMS?

a) Black and green
b) Black and red
c) Green and red
d) Violet and black

(Answer on page 154)

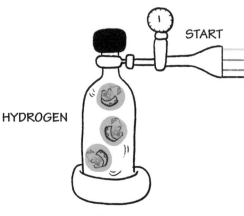

HYDROGEN

START

HYDROGEN CANISTER

To the Moon in a blink of an eye   Quiz

To calculate speed, you need a distance and the time it takes to cover that distance. **Protons** in the **LHC** ring travel at almost the **speed of light**, but do you know how fast that is? If you think that light travels almost...

a) 300,000 kilometres (186,000 miles) in a single second, flip the top corner of this page.

b) 300 kilometres (186 miles) in a single second, flip the top corner of the opposite page.

(Hint: The **protons** cross the Swiss-French borders about 70,000 times per second! At this speed, it would take these **protons** a little bit more than one second to go all the way to the Moon, because the average distance between the Earth and the Moon is 384,403 kilometres [238,857 miles].)

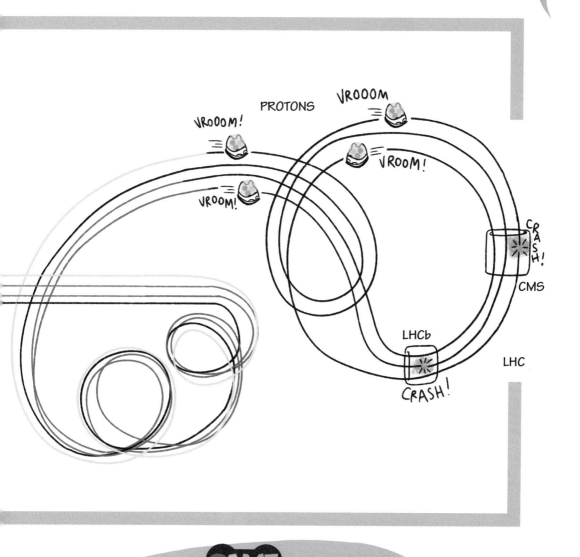

GAME

Nine is nice

Shade all the numbers that are divisible by nine to reveal the page number to go to next. (Need help? Turn to page 154.)

73	9	18	60	19	90	9	45	63
18	33	19	54	37	63	75	26	47
22	53	37	27	15	36	61	89	55
12	55	86	36	28	18	54	63	90
93	89	45	43	37	72	11	78	9
58	72	29	82	53	9	66	58	63
27	66	77	98	74	81	59	44	54
36	90	81	9	43	27	45	9	18

The first slide is projected on the screen and the title reads: "New discoveries in **dark matter** physics".

"What's **dark matter**?" you ask Loris.

"We aren't sure, but we know that it is very abundant in the Universe," replies Loris. And he reveals: "You know, the mystery surrounding **dark matter** inspired me to study **particle physics**."

"Oh, really?" you say.

"Well, we understand only 5% of the Universe. This corresponds to all the matter that we know of, including all the stars and galaxies. You see, there is still so much to explore and discover!" exclaims Loris with a twinkle in his eyes.

"Only 5%? What's the other 95% then?" you ask, puzzled.

"We think it is **dark matter** and **dark energy**," Loris replies.

DARK MATTER PARTICLE (maybe?)

"Hee hee... it sounds spooky," you chuckle.

"We haven't been able to catch **dark matter** yet, but I love the feeling of having a scientific breakthrough at my fingertips," Loris is about to explain to you all he knows about this topic and you are eager to launch into a shower of questions, but the conference starts and silence falls in the big room.

98

Now head to page 83.

The student is going to tell you something important. If you don't play your adventure is over. Flip the corner of the other page.

Great! Now you can use the **bike** to cycle to the LHCb **detector**, but have you ever wondered how this simple means of transport works? There is some **physics** behind it too.

Science Byte

Bike science: How does a bicycle stay upright?

Believe it or not, there is not a definitive explanation.

The first theory is the gyroscopic effect, which occurs when the spinning front wheel keeps rotating around its axis for a while. You can also see this phenomenon when you roll a coin vertically or play with a spinning top. The second theory involves the little steering movements of the handlebars to the left and right that riders do to help balance themselves.

But what if there is no cyclist on the bike? Imagine launching a bike by giving it a good push. As long as it is moving fast enough, but not too fast, the bike is likely to remain upright for several metres without tipping. The gyroscopic effect of the front wheel has been traditionally used to explain this phenomenon. The surprise came in 2011 when some researchers built a special riderless bike without any gyroscopic effect that could still balance itself. They showed that other parameters, like the distribution of mass and the design of the bike, contribute to its stability in quite a complicated way.

Now pedal over to page 86.

Later in the day, you write a lot of **postcards** to your friends and family while resting on a **120-metre-long** bench under some chestnut trees. The locals call it: *la Marronnier de la Treille*. They claim this to be the world's **longest** wooden bench.

Write your best friend's name and address here.

Hi! Today, Cheepy and I saw the world's biggest flower clock. See you soon!

Sign your name here.

PS: I have a chocolatey present for you!

After a **satisfying** meal of raclette cheese and potatoes, you decide to go for a stroll to digest your dinner and burn those **extra** calories. Your walk takes you into the **heart** of Geneva, where you end up at the front of the entrance to a joyful park. A sign at the gate reads: *"Parc des Bastions"*.

"Cheepy, shall we take a walk inside this park?" you ask your feathered friend.

"Cheep-cheep!" is Cheepy's positive reply.

"Great, let's go!" you say.

On the right side of the tree-lined path, you notice a wall with four solemn **statues**. It is the *Mur des Réformateur,* another famous sightseeing spot in Geneva.

"Let's take a **selfie** here!" you say to Cheepy.

The statues are 5 metres high, but Cheepy is happier to look at them from below. You know that your pet is afraid of heights; that's why he never flies more than a metre above your head.

Then, towards the end of the promenade, you bump into a group of people standing in front of a **giant chessboard** with plastic chess pieces.

"Do you want to play a game of chess with me?" asks a **young person** who looks like a student.

What do you reply?

- You reply, "Yes, I would love to!" – Flip the top corner of this page.

- You reply, "No, thank you. It is getting late…" – Flip the top corner of the opposite page.

Of course you accept. You love chess. Go to page 120.

You head towards **Building 2** to meet your new team. Well, that's easier said than done! This place is a **maze** of long corridors covered in posters of past, present and future physics conferences. There are so many offices, desks and researchers everywhere. You wonder what research or project they are working on.

The numbering of buildings does not seem to follow any recognisable pattern or order. You start at Building 33, then you pass through Building 5, and before you know it, you are now in Building 4, which is connected to Building 53 and Building 58. You wonder if anybody has ever been **lost** for so long that they were never found again. If not, you hope not to be the first one.

START

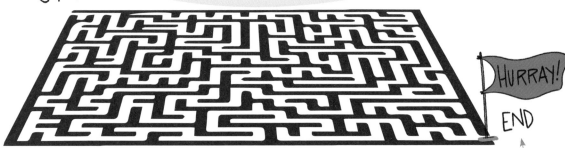

HURRAY!

END

Can you find your way? If you are lost, have a look at page 155.

With a sigh of **relief**, you see that Building 2 is just after Building 52 and that a friendly-looking young man is walking in your direction.

"Hi! You must be ……………………………………… [insert your name here], right?" he asks.

"Yes," you nod happily.

"My name is **Loris**. Congratulations on winning your school's science competition!" Loris says with a big smile.

"Thank you!" you reply.

102

"I will be your CERN **buddy** for today. To begin, I will give you a **tour** so you can familiarise yourself with this research institute. Feel free to ask me any questions. I will try to answer, if I can," says Loris.

As you take a walk with Loris around CERN, you admire the fact that the roads are named after the **great scientists** of the past, like Marie Curie.

Science Byte

Who was Marie Curie?

Marie Curie (1867–1934) was the first person to win two **Nobel Prizes**, one in Chemistry and one in Physics. She studied radioactivity in thorium and uranium, and discovered radioactive substances, such as polonium and radium.

Together with her husband, she used radium as a source of X-rays and created a small X-ray machine to help save lives during World War One. Unfortunately, in those days, the side effects of continued radiation exposure were not known, so Marie and her family handled radioactive materials without any safety precautions.

Today, X-rays are used carefully for some medical issues, such as broken bones and cancer. And, more recently, scientists have discovered that they can also use **protons** to treat cancer.

> Nothing in the world is to be feared... only understood.

Loris invites you to join a lecture in the **auditorium**—a large room used for conferences. Here, the discovery of a **new** particle, the **Higgs boson**, was announced on 4 July 2012.

Go to page 98.

HIGGS BOSON

You park your car near the data centre. The minute you put your feet on the ground just outside the vehicle, Schrödy comes to purr and rub against your legs.

Why do cats purr? Can they roar?

The truth is that no one knows for sure why cats purr. They purr when they are happy or hungry. When cats are feeling nervous or anxious, they may purr as a way to soothe themselves. It is also part of the bonding between mother cat and kittens, like a reassuring lullaby. Animals that purr cannot roar: according to some scientists, it all depends on a little bone near the vocal cords. In big cats, like lions and tigers, this bone is flexible, which enables them to emit scary roars. In cats, this bone is completely solid, so they can only purr. There is one exception: the snow leopard, which has a flexible bone but cannot roar. And have you ever heard the cheetahs? They don't roar; they… chirp.

"Hello, dear Schrödy! You look so peaceful. Sorry I don't have any food for you today and I am in a rush," you tell him.

You give him a cuddle and **hurry** towards the glass doors of the data centre. Quite disappointed, the cat starts to flick his tail back and forth.

104

Go to page 60.

These special coloured contact lenses mask your irises and reflect light.

As a result, the eye scanner **does not** recognise you, and the gate does not open. Mr Hacktosis finds you **useless** and hits you over the head with a stick. That's not the best ending... Better to continue without these special contact lenses on page 35.

Did you find Ms A.G. on page 90?

➔ If you did, continue reading.

➔ If not, have another look on pages 90–91. (Need help? Turn to page 151.)

You rush over to Ms A.G. and shake her hand vigorously.

"Ms A.G., I am **so glad** to see you! I **really** need your help! Someone hacked Prof. Virtualli's computer," you say in one breath.

"Oh no, that's **terrible!**" worries Ms A.G.

"Now I need his password to stop the hacker," you say, panting.

"Prof. Virtualli told me that one letter of the password is: **H**," Ms A.G. whispers in your ear.

"Ok! And what about the rest?" you ask, feeling very hopeful.

"He hid them in **five** different places at CERN: SM18, the data centre, the **antimatter** factory, ALICE **detector** and the part of the **LHC** tunnel between ALICE and ATLAS," she lists in a low voice.

"That's great! Thank you very much!" you say with a **huge** sigh of relief.

As you are about to leave, she adds, "Prof. Virtualli also said to type the fourth letter 10 times and to add a face with a tongue sticking out at the end," giving a small shrug.

You got one piece of the password and some useful information, but you still need the other five letters. With no time to dilly-dally, you rush to the next destination: **SM18**. Check where it is on the map (pages 2–3) before you continue.

List of the locations to find the password:
· ·

- CCC
- SM18
- data centre
- **antimatter** factory
- ALICE **detector**
- **LHC** tunnel between ALICE and ATLAS

Additional information:
· ·

- Type the fourth letter 10 times.
- Add a face with a tongue sticking out at the end.

SM18 is bustling with people moving and testing long blue tubes. These contain the SUPER powerful LHC magnets, which are about 1000 times stronger than your fridge magnets. These big instruments control the direction of the tiny protons.

Let's peek inside the blue tubes. Protons fly through these two pipes, which are surrounded by magnets.

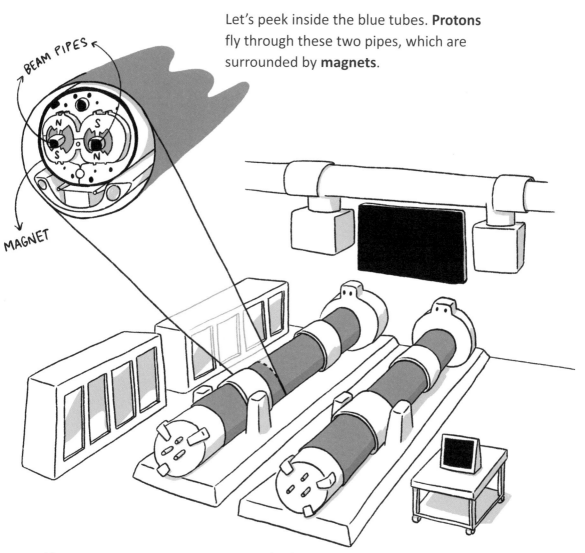

BEAM PIPES

MAGNET

If you want to see a sweet surprise, check out the bonus material on page 159.

Turn the page to continue the adventure.

Curiously CERN

How to control a particle's steering wheel?

Protons normally travel in straight lines, but magnets bend their paths. This trick works well with protons, because they are positively charged, as well as with other particles that have a positive or negative charge. Neutral particles, like neutrons, keep the same trajectory despite the magnets.

The LHC accelerator has more than 1200 magnets to make the protons fly in a circular path, following the shape of the LHC ring.

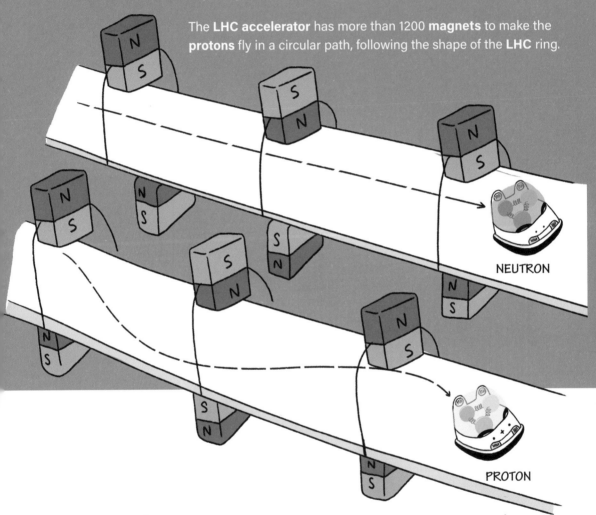

NEUTRON

PROTON

LHC magnets are electromagnets; they are magnetic only if electric current passes through them. On the contrary, fridge magnets are not electromagnets; they always stick to the door of the fridge, even when there is a power cut. Fridge magnets are permanent magnets.

Science Byte

Electromagnets around you

Beyond **particle accelerators**, **electromagnets** of all sizes are used widely and in many common devices around you, for example:

- in electric bells and buzzers
- in loudspeakers and headphones
- in junkyard cranes that lift old cars off the ground
- in computers
- in hospital instruments used to see inside the body, like the MRI (magnetic resonance imaging) scanners
- in superfast Maglev (magnetic levitation) trains, which travel without touching the ground.

Quiz

Can you transform a nail into an electromagnet?

It is easy! You just need a long nail, a battery and a copper wire. When the copper wire is connected to the positive (+) and negative (−) terminals of the battery, electric **current** flows though the wire, and the nail becomes magnetic. The more times you wrap the wire around the nail, the stronger your **magnet**. So, which is the right way to assemble the nail, battery and wire? (Answer on page 151)

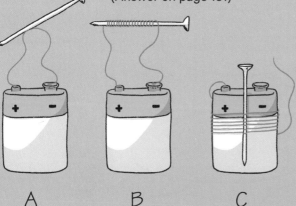

A   B   C

Find out what makes the **LHC magnets** special before continuing your search for the next letter.

Go to page 74.

If you choose to be a student...

"How much longer?" you ask your parents.

"About one hour, sweetheart," replies your mum.

After five minutes that felt like **five centuries**, you complain again, "How much longer? I really cannot wait!" You've never liked long road trips.

After an hour on the road, you arrive at your destination. Your heart is **thumping**, like a drum in your chest. Curious by nature, visiting CERN is your **dream** come true. You had won a science competition organised by your school, and now you have the chance to spend a week exploring this research centre. You are over the moon!

Your mum plants a kiss on your forehead and your dad gives you a big hug. You stand tall and smile, ready for **the best week** of your student life.

"Take advantage of this opportunity!" reminds your dad.

"I will!" you reply.

This is your chance to find answers to questions that have been literally **fizzing** in your mind: What is **particle physics**? What are the unsolved mysteries of our Universe? What are CERN researchers doing all day long?

Do you have any other science-related questions that have always fascinated you? Ones that even your parents cannot answer? Write them below.

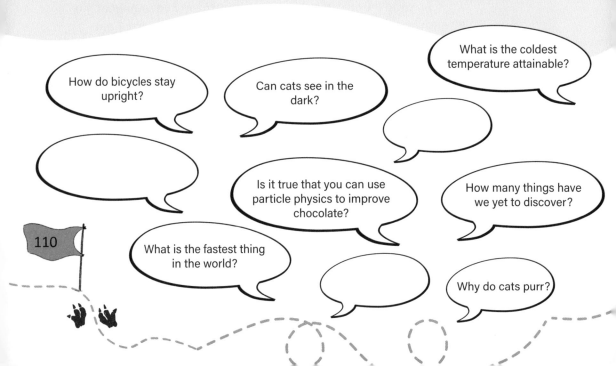

What is the coldest temperature attainable?

How do bicycles stay upright?

Can cats see in the dark?

Is it true that you can use particle physics to improve chocolate?

How many things have we yet to discover?

What is the fastest thing in the world?

Why do cats purr?

Your experience at CERN will be riddled with some **unbelievable challenges**. A helper and a couple of tools might come in handy—or not, who knows... Anyway, you have nothing to lose.

Choose your helper

○ *Frankenstein's* monster

○ An animal trainer

○ A Swiss chef

Choose your tools

Pick two of the following:

○ A bottle of champagne

○ An inflatable balloon

○ A compass

○ A Swiss watch

Tip: Put a tick next to your choices!

Of course, I recommend the Swiss chef.

Now you are ready to start. Turn the page and **good luck!**

A week ago, you received an email saying that your visit to CERN starts at the **reception**.

CERN's bustling reception is a **flurry** of activity. Around you, all kinds of people are mingling: crowds of **students** on school trips, groups of physics teachers on training courses, packs of **tourists** waiting for a CERN tour, business people with expensive wristwatches, a pair of **journalists** setting up microphones, **researchers** from every country in the world, and all sorts of creative people who want to get inspired by the quirks of the **particle** world.

"**Welcome** to CERN! I am sure you will have a great experience here," the receptionist says and gives you some instructions on how to collect your CERN access card. Needless to say, you do not waste a minute. You go to the card office, take a photo, and then wear your freshly-printed card around your neck with pride.

The phenomenal **Photon**: Light, waves inside your microwave oven, radio waves and X-rays are made up of **photons**.

The dazzling **Dark Matter**: Researchers are looking high and low for it, but they haven't managed to find it yet.

The hilarious **Higgs boson**: Its discovery was announced here at CERN in 2012.

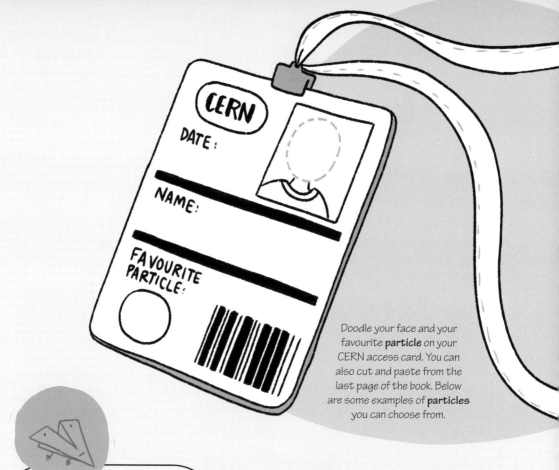

Doodle your face and your favourite **particle** on your CERN access card. You can also cut and paste from the last page of the book. Below are some examples of **particles** you can choose from.

The exciting **Electron**: It is found in clouds that surround the **nucleus** of an **atom**.

The prodigious **Proton**: It runs inside the **LHC accelerator**, but can also be found in the **nucleus** of **atoms**. It contains glorious **Gluons**, which keep the **nucleus** together like glue, and quirky **Quarks**.

The magnificent **Muon**: It's the big cousin of the **electron**, about 200 times heavier.

Now you are ready to go to page 102.

In SM18, the **magnets** are tested at low temperatures before they are lowered into the **LHC** tunnel, 100 metres underground. It is a big workshop area, so where could this piece of the password be hidden?

A cheerful technician walks towards you: "Hi! You must be looking for a letter, right?" he asks.

"How did you know that?" you wonder.

"Oh, that's a secret. Anyway, before Prof. Virtualli died, he gave me these instructions: Stay in this exact position and empty your wallet," he adds.

"Eh?!? Okay..." you reply, sounding a bit doubtful.

If your desk is messy, your wallet is even worse: tickets, bills, business cards, credit cards, money from all over the world, sticky notes... You look lost.

"A banknote of 200 Swiss francs can help you," says the man with a chuckle. "Hold it horizontally upright in front of you and follow the thumb..." he trails off without completing his sentence.

Luckily, you happen to have one banknote of 200 Swiss francs in your wallet. It is a lot of money, but you always keep it in your wallet for another reason: the images on this banknote are dedicated to CERN.

Quiz

What's the image on the banknote showing?

a) A **particle** collision

b) The explosion of a star in a galaxy far away

c) An erupting volcano

(Answer on page 151)

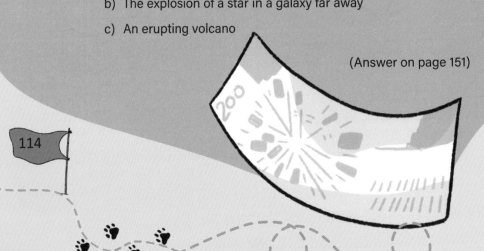

On the other side of the banknote, you can see an illustration of a right hand with the thumb and index finger forming an **L**, and the middle finger pointing out.

What's the funky hand gesture on this Swiss banknote?

Curiously CERN

It's not a new, trendy hand gesture, but a handy rule to understand what's going on when moving **particles (protons)** are brought close to the **LHC magnets**. The **particles** would fly straight ahead, but the **magnets** bend their paths, so they can follow the shape of the **LHC** ring. The position of the index finger follows the direction (velocity) of the **particles**, the middle finger represents the direction of the **magnetic field** and the position of the thumb is the force that acts on the **particles** to bend their pathway.

You turn the banknote horizontally upright in front of you and follow the thumb's direction. **Bingo!** There you spot a piece of paper with a letter written on it. It's the letter "**E**".

You want to thank the technician, but he has vanished. Anyway, now it is time to drive to the **data centre**, where all the data from CERN are stored and another letter of the password is hidden.

Go to page 104.

Maybe this **dinosaur** is not angry but just **hungry**, you think. Rather than eating you or other humans, it could enjoy some **local** delights, such as *moitié-moitié* cheese fondue, Swiss chocolate or a dino-sized portion of raclette.

It may not be the smartest idea, but why not give it a try. Just the smell of **melted cheese** could keep the **dinosaur** away for a while, or maybe this **dinosaur** has a sweet tooth. Who knows...

A **pompous chef** is at your service and reads his menu out loud, overemphasising each word. Choose three dishes while he reads.

"Can you quickly prepare a cheese fondue, ... [insert the dish of your first choice], ... [insert your second choice] and .... [insert your third choice]?" you ask impatiently.

"Yes! Sure!" replies the chef.

Right away he mixes the **ingredients** in some huge pots of an improvised camping kitchen. Meanwhile, you try to gain some time by distracting the **dinosaur** with a perilous **hide-and-seek** game.

"Voilà!" says the chef, showing his excellent work with pride.

Both of you leave the dishes behind and run a few metres away to see if the **dinosaur** is attracted to the food. You have a **niggling** feeling that this trick is not going to work, but you never know.

MENU

Moitié-moitié cheese fondue

A pot of delicious melted cheese, traditionally Gruyère cheese and Vacherin Fribourgeois cheese, scooped with pieces of bread

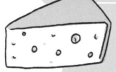

Raclette

A copious portion of melted cheese accompanied with potatoes

Rösti

A traditional dish of the German-speaking part of Switzerland made with grated potatoes

Chocolate

Did you know that the Swiss are the world's largest consumer of chocolate?

Malakoff

Fried beignets with cheese filling

Longeole

A traditional pork sausage with cumin

Cardon Genevois

Pickled cardoon stalks, a vegetable relatively unknown outside Geneva

Bircher müsli

Oats soaked in milk, yogurt and fruits, as an ideal, filling breakfast

Meringue à la double crème

Meringues with double cream, for a full fat, full sugar yummy dessert

Turn the page.

Sorry to say that this food does not deter the **dinosaur** from advancing towards you and the chef. Being a carnivorous **dinosaur**, it is probably more interested in eating you than a tasty cheese fondue.

"This **dinosaur** does not appreciate my culinary art," complains the chef, annoyed by the entire situation. "*C'est pas possible!* It's not possible!"

"Eat my food!" he shouts. "Or I'll make a BBQ out of you!" This is not the best thing to say to an aggressive **dinosaur**, you think, shaking your head.

Now you notice that a flock of sheep is grazing nearby and does not seem to care about the prehistoric predator. Equally, the **dinosaur** does not seem to notice the flock but insists on sprinting towards you and the chef.

The chef runs for the hills, dropping all his ingredients in haste.

Go to page 19 before it is too late.

118

You **inflate** the balloon and rub it on your **wool** sweater for at least 15 seconds. Then you hold the balloon a couple of centimetres above the salt and pepper mixture without touching it. The pepper **jumps off** and sticks onto the balloon leaving the salt behind. Brilliant!

Pepper & Salt

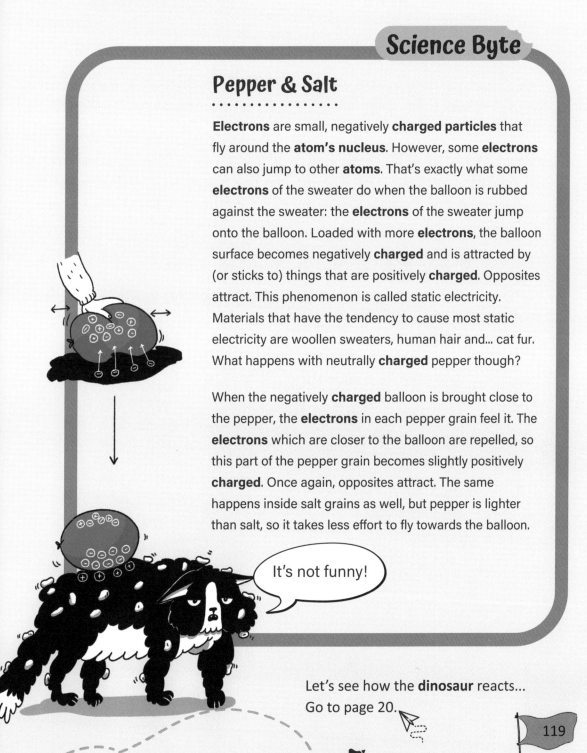

Electrons are small, negatively **charged particles** that fly around the **atom's nucleus**. However, some **electrons** can also jump to other **atoms**. That's exactly what some **electrons** of the sweater do when the balloon is rubbed against the sweater: the **electrons** of the sweater jump onto the balloon. Loaded with more **electrons**, the balloon surface becomes negatively **charged** and is attracted by (or sticks to) things that are positively **charged**. Opposites attract. This phenomenon is called static electricity. Materials that have the tendency to cause most static electricity are woollen sweaters, human hair and... cat fur. What happens with neutrally **charged** pepper though?

When the negatively **charged** balloon is brought close to the pepper, the **electrons** in each pepper grain feel it. The **electrons** which are closer to the balloon are repelled, so this part of the pepper grain becomes slightly positively **charged**. Once again, opposites attract. The same happens inside salt grains as well, but pepper is lighter than salt, so it takes less effort to fly towards the balloon.

It's not funny!

Let's see how the **dinosaur** reacts... Go to page 20.

While playing, you notice that your playmate's sweater has a **curious design** with some lines that seem to originate from a point in the centre. It looks a bit like a firework explosion, but not quite.

"You have an interesting sweater. Did you buy it in Geneva?" you ask while moving the knight piece.

"Yes, it shows **particle** collisions. I bought it at CERN," says the student.

"Ah, CERN!" you exclaim. "Did you meet **Prof. Virtualli**? He was my grandfather; he used to work there. Unfortunately, I've never understood what CERN researchers do exactly."

"Well, I am not an expert either, but I know that people at CERN study the **origin of matter**—what happened just after the **Big Bang**. Imagine running the clock backwards, not by one hour or two, but by **13.8 billion years!** What would you see?" asks the student.

"I don't know, but it sounds fascinating," you say.

"CERN is a unique place. If you have time, I highly recommend a visit. It is just a tram-ride away!" suggests the student.

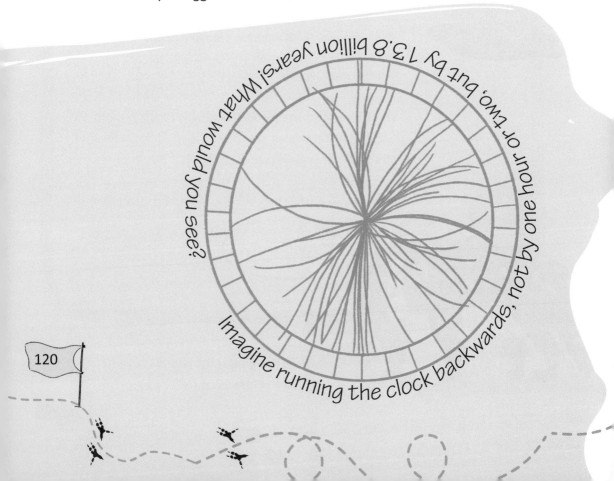

You have never been to a **research institute** and you would like to have a look.

"What do you think, Cheepy?" you ask your travel companion.

Cheepy chirps happily.

Time flies, and you quickly win the match. Actually, you are unbeatable at chess. You have never lost a match in your life.

You go to sleep dreaming about tomorrow, while poor Cheepy's dreams (or rather, **nightmares**) are populated by scary-looking animals—kittens that transform into tigers, turtles that roar and **dinosaurs** that come alive—all lurking around Geneva city centre.

Curiously CERN
BIG BAAAANG? What's that?
. . . .

If you are thinking that the expression **"Big Bang"** does not sound so scientific, you are quite right. The astronomer Sir Fred Hoyle invented the name during an interview on the radio. He was actually making a comment against the **Big Bang** theory and was supporting an alternative idea.

Over the years, however, more and more evidence piled up in favour of the **Big Bang** theory, and the funny name stuck. Now we know that the whole Universe is around 13.8 billion years old and that at the beginning, it was super dense and hot. As it expanded, it cooled down.

The **LHC accelerator** smashes together **particles** at great energies, creating the conditions that existed at the start of the Universe, just a fraction of a second after the **Big Bang.**

Turn the page.

Next morning, you are ready for a great day. Cheepy, on the other hand, is not in the best shape after all those **horrible** nightmares. After breakfast, you take the tram that goes to CERN. Cheepy is sitting on your shoulder. He is a well-behaved bird, and he is used to taking public transport.

It's peak hour and there are only **two** free seats. Where do you sit?

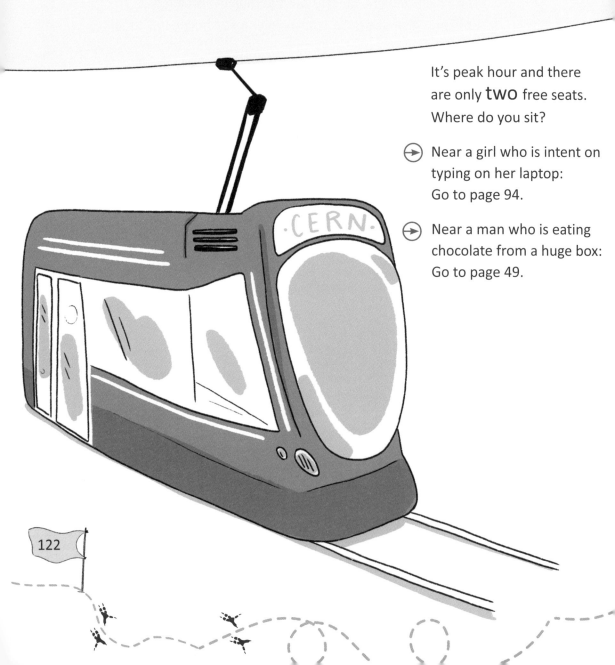

→ Near a girl who is intent on typing on her laptop: Go to page 94.

→ Near a man who is eating chocolate from a huge box: Go to page 49.

You do not have any champagne, so you decide to **steal** a bottle that you see in someone's office. Too bad that you get **caught** red-handed. This champagne was a thank-you present that the physicists wanted to give to the people working at the **CERN Control Centre**, or the CCC. Everybody gets so mad at you, but after you explain that you were trying to save the day, they agree to give you the bottle.

Hold the bottle securely and proceed gingerly to page 143.

You decide to go to the CERN restaurant. Maybe some food will give you some **energy** to think. This restaurant at CERN is usually bustling with people, but today it is completely **deserted**, except for one person who looks like a **tourist**.

Feeling hopeless, you bury your head in your hands. Suddenly, a bird glides along the entire length of the restaurant, dropping a wad of paper from its beak not far from where you are sitting.

You collect the paper from the floor. With your eyes **wide** open, you exclaim: "It's the missing letter of the password. It is the letter E!"

The only other person present in the restaurant jumps for joy and shouts in the direction of the bird: "**Cheeeeeeepy!**"

"Cheepy?" you whisper to yourself. Coincidentally, you realise that you have **all** the letters of the word "Cheepy". You type it quickly on Prof. Virtualli's laptop, remembering to type the fourth letter 10 times and add a face with a tongue sticking out.

Tongue Out Quiz

Can you see a face sticking the tongue out among these emoticons?

a) : -)

b) : - P

c) : - (

ENTER PASSWORD TO CONTINUE:

d) •w•

e) (⊥o⊥)

(Check if you've entered the correct password on page 153.)

"**Unbelievable,**" you mumble to yourself. "**IT WORKS!**" you heave a sigh of relief. Now you can **finally** stop the work of the hacker. The robot mice freeze and the **dinosaur** comes to a sudden halt.

Beat the hacker

Hackers can easily guess short words, birthdays, dictionary words and commonly used passwords like: 123456789 and qwerty. The word CHEEPY has only six letters and is also listed in English dictionaries: a hacker would crack it in less than one second. The longer the password, the more difficult it is to guess it! Having a mix of letters, numbers and symbols is the best. When you need to create a password, check if it's strong enough on password strength checker websites that you can readily find online.

The longer the password, the more difficult it is to guess it!

Congratulations! You have accomplished your mission, but don't you feel a bit clueless about what really happened?

How could that bird carry the right piece of the password? How could this mysterious person in the cafeteria shout the right password to you?

And why was the student pouring expensive champagne into a big bucket?

Go to page 110 to find out.

Go to page 10 to uncover the mystery.

Have you completed all the three stories? Go to the epilogue on page 148.

Then, all of a sudden, everything goes black. Two eyes gleam out of the darkness... They are Schrödy's. But where is Cheepy? Hopefully not inside the cat's mouth.

Do cats see in the dark?

Yes, cats' eyes are more sensitive to dim light compared to human eyes. A cat's pupil can look like a vertical line during the day, but it expands at night, allowing more light to enter. Light—which is made of **photons**—is absorbed by some cells in the eyes, called rods. The glow-in-the-dark effect of cats' eyes is caused by the *tapetum lucidum*: this is like a mirror at the back of the eye which enhances the amount of light that the rods can perceive. Night vision helps cats to hunt in the dusk and dawn. Poor Cheepy is in danger.

Turn the page.

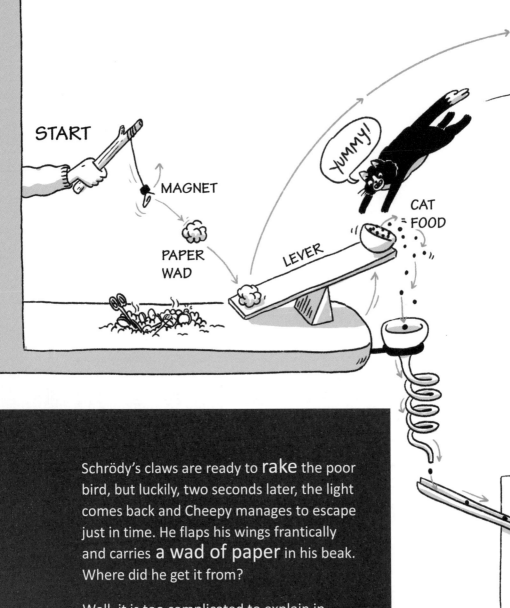

START

MAGNET

PAPER
WAD

LEVER

YUMMY!

CAT
FOOD

Schrödy's claws are ready to **rake** the poor bird, but luckily, two seconds later, the light comes back and Cheepy manages to escape just in time. He flaps his wings frantically and carries **a wad of paper** in his beak. Where did he get it from?

Well, it is too complicated to explain in words... See why in this picture above.

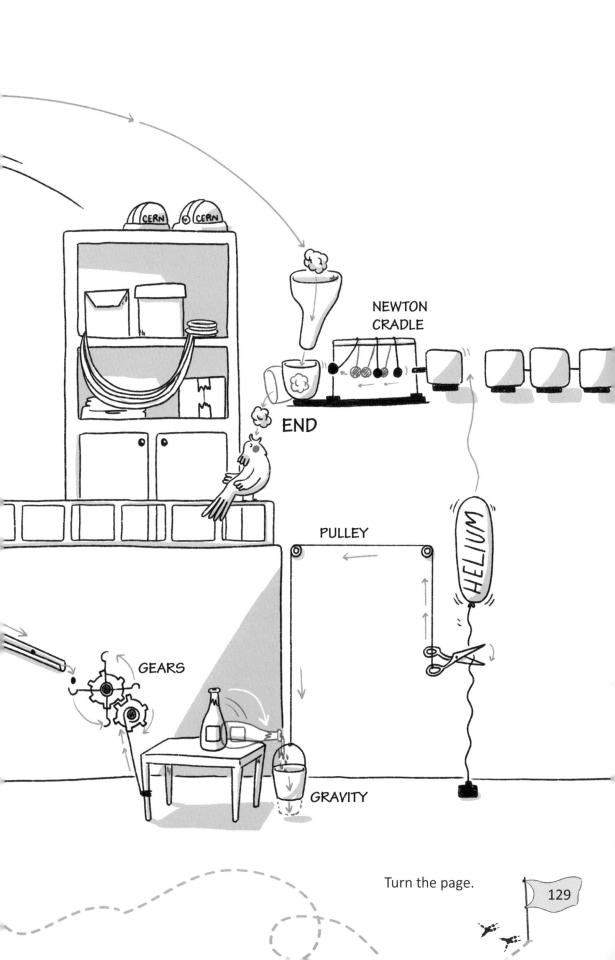

CERN CERN

NEWTON
CRADLE

END

PULLEY

HELIUM

GEARS

GRAVITY

Turn the page.

The cat is still on his tail, so Cheepy flies out of the **antimatter** factory, and you quickly hop into your trusty double-decker bus to follow behind. Just outside the building, you encounter an enormous pair of feet, accompanied by a whipping tail and a threatening roar: a **towering dinosaur** is standing in front of you.

"Good heavens! This is a great idea for a carnival parade, but isn't it a bit too early for the *Mardi Gras* parties?" you think.

While you are wondering about this sight, Cheepy swoops past the **ferocious dinosaur** just inches away from its eyes and flies towards the south of CERN's main site.

Too bad that a flock of **sheep** is obstructing the road and the double-decker bus you are driving is stuck. You honk the horn a couple of times, but the sheep are not in a hurry.

"Cheepy, I need to wait for the sheep to move away, let's meet at the CERN restaurant," you shout to Cheepy. **"Head South-East!"**

"*Cheep-cheep*" he replies.

While waiting for the sheep to move out of the way, you have a closer look at the **dinosaur**. You start to think that it is real. You decide to call your best friend, Robert. He knows absolutely **everything** about each and every **dinosaur** that walked on this planet. He has memorised all the names, diets and bone structures of every animal of the prehistoric world. If **dinosaurs** wore shoes, he would definitely know their shoe sizes too. Now you can just picture in your mind a T-Rex walking in high heels.

"Hi, how's it going?" answers Robert on the other side of the line.

"Hi, Robert! I think there is a **dinosaur** in front of me," you confess abruptly.

"Eh?!?!?! What?!?" exclaims Robert, trying to suppress his laughter.

"Yes! Too bad my phone's camera is broken, so I can't show you," you say.

"Hey, did you hit your head somewhere? Are you okay?" asks your friend, now with a worried voice.

"Actually, I almost fell from a crane. Luckily a **firefighter** saved me and rescued Cheepy. Now I am waiting for some sheep to move out of my way so that the double-decker bus I'm driving can pass. Well, it is a long story…" you explain all in one breath.

"Double-decker bus? Sheep? Crane? Wow, sounds like an adventure! I am looking forward to hearing all your stories as soon as you are back. But don't worry about **dinosaurs**, okay? They went **extinct** about 65 million years ago!" Robert points out.

"Yeah… that's true, I guess. It must be a carnival chariot then…" you suggest, still slightly unconvinced.

"It could be. By the way, have you visited Dinoplagne?" he asks.

"No, I am going there tomorrow!" you reply.

"Great! You can learn a lot about **dinosaurs** there," says Robert.

DINOPLAGNE

Turn the page.

Science Byte

To be precise, not all dinosaurs went extinct

Modern birds, including Cheepy, are avian **dinosaurs**. Birds descended from a group of two-legged, meat-eating **dinosaurs** known as theropods. That's the same group as the towering *Tyrannosaurus rex* and the smaller *Velociraptor*.

Giant lizards?

Initially, most people thought that **dinosaurs** looked like giant lizards. More and more discoveries, however, have transformed the way palaeontologists (that is, **dinosaur** experts) think about **dinosaurs'** appearance, behaviour and lifestyle. For example, several feathered **dinosaurs**, like the *Dilong paradoxus*, were discovered in China, and the well-preserved tail of a feathered **dinosaur** was found inside an amber stone in Myanmar.

We are dinosaurs too!

If you want to surprise your friends with an edible **dinosaur**, check out the bonus material on page 161.

Finally, the road is clear and you head straight to the restaurant.

The place is empty. You can only see a desperate-looking **researcher**.

Every minute that passes, you feel increasingly nervous for the fate of your friend.

Just then, Cheepy flies into the restaurant and lands straight on top of your head, finding comfort on your wool knit hat. A moment of pure joy!

"Cheeeeeepy!" you cry in happiness. "Please, never leave me again!"

You turn back at the researcher who is now beaming. What a rapid change of mood!

Why is this researcher suddenly so happy?

Do you want to discover what all this fuss is about **dinosaurs**?

Go to page 44 and play the role of a CERN researcher to find out!

Go to page 110 and play the role of a student.

Have you completed all the three stories? Go to the epilogue on page 148.

Fizzling facts

. . . .

If you examine a glass filled with champagne, you will notice that the rising bubbles form streams, each beginning at a certain starting point in the glass. This point is normally a small, even invisible scratch or imperfection on the inner surface of the glass. Here, bubbles can form easily from the reaction between water and carbon dioxide **molecules**.

What happens if you add salt to champagne? Salt grains consist of small crystals, each having numerous edges, meaning that the carbon dioxide suddenly has many more points to react with water. Because of this, more bubbles develop and rise to the top of the glass. The reaction ends when the salt grains dissolve in the liquid and the many sharp edges disappear.

You turn your attention back to the **dinosaur**... You need to come up with another plan, hopefully a winning one!

This time, you decide to consult your helper, the one you chose on page 111.

→ If you chose a Swiss chef, go to page 116.

→ If you chose an animal trainer, go to page 53.

→ If you chose *Frankenstein's monster*, go to page 145.

As soon as you exit the **antimatter** factory, you come face to face with a **dinosaur!** The impressive jaws of the prehistoric beast reveal teeth as sharp as **blades**, and the movements are super **realistic**. "It must be a performance for the children of CERN kindergarten," you think. "But isn't it a bit **too scary** for little children?" you ask yourself.

Not far from the **dinosaur**, a young person, who looks like a **student**, is pouring expensive **champagne** into a big bucket. This is so weird, but you don't have time to waste. Thinking that today is officially the **craziest** day of your life, you get into your car and drive to the **ALICE detector**. Check the directions on the map (pages 2–3), then turn the page.

The ALICE **detector** is 100 metres underground and its entrance at ground level is protected by a **security system** that blocks **intruders** from accessing the elevator.

You are heading towards that gate when all of a sudden, a hand brutally **grabs** your neck from behind.

"I want **all** the letters you've collected so far," **booms** a man viciously as he lunges from the shadows. This man must be the hacker. He is not well-intentioned, so you figure it's **better** to give him what he wants.

"I have collected the letters: H, E and C. But how did you know that the next piece of the password would be here?" you ask, baffled.

"I threatened Ms A.G.," replies the hacker arrogantly. His breath is terrible and smells so rank. You don't know the hacker's name, and obviously this is not the best moment to exchange pleasantries, so you will go for **Mr Hacktosis** (the combination of the words "hacker" and "halitosis", which means bad breath).

"What did you do?!?!? And how did you get my phone number and Ms A.G.'s in the first place?" you question without hiding your shock.

"In all modesty… I **hacked** both your phones," says Mr Hacktosis with a deliberately nasty glint in his eyes. He emits another **nauseating** whiff, but you try to stay focused. "Your password is your date of birth. It was so easy to guess…"

"What?!?! Why are you doing all this?" you shout.

"I get a thrill out of seeing the fear in people's eyes," replies Mr Hacktosis with a disgusting grin on his face. "Haven't you seen my great dinosaur robot around? It's the most realistic dinosaur robot on the planet— perfect in every detail and every movement," he boasts while you wish to pinch your nose with both your hands to cope with the stench.

"Are you saying that there is a dinosaur robot roaming freely around Geneva?" you ask, afraid of what Mr Hacktosis might say.

"Galloping, not roaming," he points out. "And I hope it will cause a bit of havoc at CERN too."

So the dinosaur you saw in front of the antimatter factory isn't part of a children's theatre, but a robot! Now it is all clear! Mr Hacktosis is building robots targeting people's fears. He started with a terrifying dinosaur, then a squeaky invasion of mice in the data centre... and no doubt he will soon create robots of menacing snakes, fierce tigers, poisonous spiders, creepy creatures, and who knows what else.

"Why are you doing that? You are just an awful human being, you can't..." you protest.

"Enough chatter! Now move!" interrupts Mr Hacktosis, pushing you towards the gate.

You have no choice but to go to page 55.

The **dinosaur** is distracted by the *Frankenstein's monster* balloon but not frightened at all. It plays with the big bag of air for a while, until it sinks its teeth into it. Disappointed, it turns its attention back to you.

It is safer to choose another option as your helper. Return to page 134.

"Calm down and think," you try to tell yourself. Turning the computer off and on does not make any difference. The same **worrying** sentence appears on the screen.

You grab your cell phone and type a message to your colleague, Odette. She shares the office with you, but she's still at the conference, **miles and miles** away. She might have experienced this problem before. Her flight is scheduled for tomorrow in the early morning, so it would be impolite to **wake** her up, but you give it a try anyway.

"Hi Odette! Sorry for disturbing at this time, but Prof. Virtualli's computer could have been hacked..."

You click the SEND button and really hope that she hasn't fallen asleep yet. Thankfully, she answers quickly:

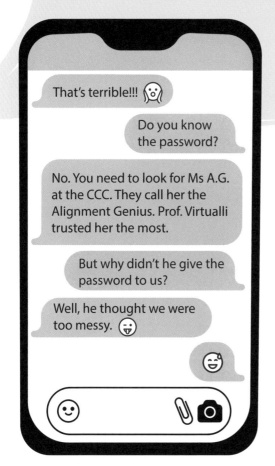

That's terrible!!! 😲

Do you know the password?

No. You need to look for Ms A.G. at the CCC. They call her the Alignment Genius. Prof. Virtualli trusted her the most.

But why didn't he give the password to us?

Well, he thought we were too messy. 😛

😅

Go to page 72.

Schrödy's **behaviour** says it all. If there were **a lot of mice** just a few metres away, the cat would not have been so **quiet**. So these mice must be **fake!**

Good thinking! There is nothing to be scared of. You realise that this is a multitude of the **most real-looking mouse robots** ever seen.

Suddenly, your phone rings and you receive a **frightening** message in capital letters from an **unknown** number: "GIVE ME THE PASSWORD!"

Someone is looking for the same password as you. It must be the hacker, who has realised that if **you** find the password, his nasty game is **over**.

A mouse darts behind the corner.

"Heeeelp!" someone is yelling.

A terrified computer expert is standing on a table full of cables and technical equipment. You can hear the **fear** in his voice.

"These are just little mouse robots, don't be afraid," you try to tell him.

"Robots?!?!?" he says, confused.

"Yes, **harmless** robots," you explain, grabbing one in your hands.

"Really?" Reeling, the man does not dare to look at them.

"I've called for help, and it'll come soon. In the meantime, do you have a **message** from Prof. Virtualli?" you ask.

He nods, extracts a wad of paper from his pocket and **throws** it to you.

"Great! I promise that this **nightmare** will be over soon," you exclaim after catching the paper.

"Thank you so much!" replied the computer expert.

The paper has a big letter "C" printed in the centre and a message on the reverse side. It's Prof. Virtualli's **unmistakable** chicken-scratch handwriting. Luckily, several years of working with him has trained you to **decipher** his handwriting. It's a weird poem:

> To Elena: ♡ ♡ ♡
> Roses are red, magnets are blue.
> I'm in a factory, and so are you.
> You're my love and the letters is concealed,
> with a paperclip made of steel.
> ♡ ♡ ♡

You read it quickly, "*To Elena: Roses are red, magnets are blue. I'm in a factory, and so are you. You're my love and the letter is concealed, with a paperclip made of steel.*" You cannot help but **explode** in laughter.

This time, the good old Prof. Virtualli gave you an excellent hint! What sounds like the worst romantic poem ever written in **human history** is a secret message. It tells you **where** to search for the next letter of the password and **how** to pick it up.

Go to page 16 to learn more about this mysterious ELENA.

141

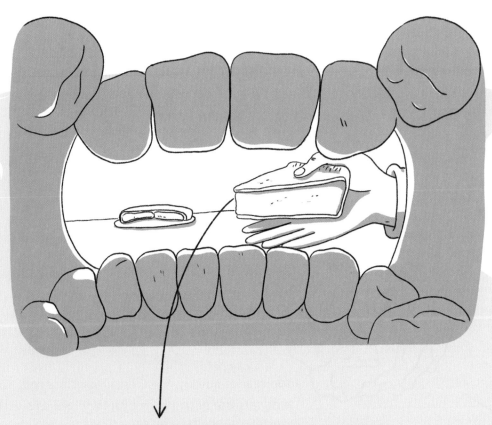

No *fève*. It isn't your lucky day today.
Choose another slice on page 59 and
try your luck again.

It's great to have a champagne bottle, but it can be tricky to open. Can you do it? You hold the cork firmly and try to pull it out of the bottle.

After an incredible champagne shower, you pour whatever liquid that is left into a big bucket, and push it as close as possible to the **dinosaur**.

Unfortunately, you've wasted a good bottle of champagne. The **dinosaur** does not seem interested in drinking this expensive beverage at all.

BEEEEEP BEEEEEP BEEEEEP

"Hi, Mum and Dad! I am quite busy at the moment," you answer the call, trying not to sound too worried.

"We just wanted to check how your day's been," explain your parents.

"Well… it's been complicated but interesting! By the way, at the next big celebration, I want to practise opening champagne bottles or any other fizzy drink. But I have to go now," you cut it short. "Bye!"

"Ok! Bye!" reply your parents in a perplexed voice.

Science Byte

Bubbling facts

To make champagne, little organisms called yeasts are added to grape juice. They eat the grape's sugar and produce alcohol and a gas, called carbon dioxide. The gas stays dissolved in the liquid, trapped under pressure inside the bottle, until someone pops the cork.

Quiz

What do you think will happen if you drop a pinch of salt into a glass full of champagne?

a) An impressive fizz: Flip the top of this page.

b) Nothing: Flip the top of the opposite page.

143

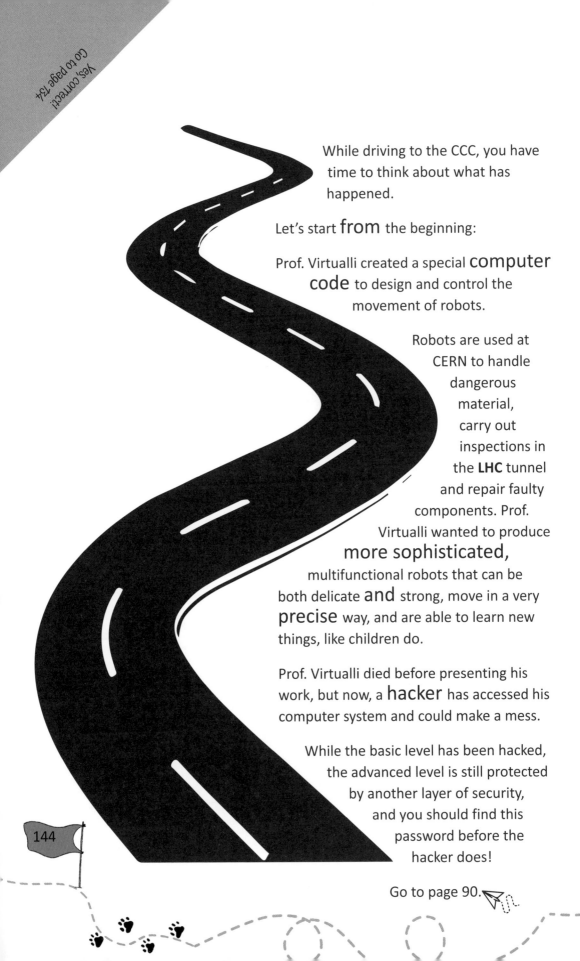

Yes, correct! Go to page 134.

While driving to the CCC, you have time to think about what has happened.

Let's start **from** the beginning:

Prof. Virtualli created a special **computer code** to design and control the movement of robots.

Robots are used at CERN to handle dangerous material, carry out inspections in the **LHC** tunnel and repair faulty components. Prof. Virtualli wanted to produce **more sophisticated,** multifunctional robots that can be both delicate **and** strong, move in a very **precise** way, and are able to learn new things, like children do.

Prof. Virtualli died before presenting his work, but now, a **hacker** has accessed his computer system and could make a mess.

While the basic level has been hacked, the advanced level is still protected by another layer of security, and you should find this password before the hacker does!

Go to page 90.

144

Frankenstein's monster is so **grotesque** that you hope it will **scare** the **dinosaur** away.

Do you know who invented Frankenstein's monster?

You can take a photo with my statue at *Plaine de Plainpalais* in the Geneva city centre.

In 1816, a British girl named Mary Shelley and her three friends spent a summer near Geneva. Due to bad weather, they were forced to stay indoors for several days. To relieve their boredom, they decided to each come up horror story. Mary's story was the best later became a successful science-fiction book. In her novel, Victor Frankenstein, a young scientist, builds a "human" from bones and body parts recovered from cemeteries and animal slaughterhouses. He brings his creation to life, but flees in horror when the monstrous creature awakens. To know how it ends, you should read the novel (if you dare). For this story, Mary might have been inspired by well-known physicists of her era—in particular, Luigi Galvani (1737–1798), who tried to resuscitate dead animals using electric **currents**.

Sorry to disappoint, but your helper is just a **giant inflatable balloon** with the appearance of *Frankenstein's monster*. Since it is as tall as the **dinosaur**, you hope it will work like a scarecrow— or in this case, a "**scaredino**".

Is the *Frankenstein's monster* balloon enough to frighten the **dinosaur**?

Turn to page 138 with your fingers crossed.

145

With a flutter of wings, Cheepy approaches the
data centre. Bounding towards the same
direction, the feline gets distracted by some
mice. Sniffing around the data centre, Schrödy
is a bit puzzled.

They look like mice but strangely do not smell of anything.

Curiously CERN

Data centre

When **protons** collide inside the **detectors**, they produce a lot of
different particles which leave traces (as you have seen on page 65).
All these traces correspond to data, which are stored in the CERN
data centre. Among all these data there could hide a new particle or
some insight into the unsolved mysteries of the Universe.

However, it takes a lot of computational power to work out what
happens inside the **detectors** and analyse these data. A single
computer cannot handle the workload, so CERN researchers have
developed the Worldwide **LHC** Computing Grid. This is a network of
computers located inside the CERN data centre and in places around
the globe: if you send a request from your computer, the process
may be carried out by computers on the other side of the planet; the
results will then return and appear on your screen.

The World Wide Web (WWW or Web)

CERN is also the birthplace of the **WWW**. The first webpage was created here by Sir Tim Berners-Lee, and you can still find it on: http://info.cern.ch/hypertext/WWW/TheProject.html. It is a very simple webpage without any colours or images.

Some people confuse the Internet with the **WWW**. The **WWW** is the collection of all the webpages and the Internet is a global network of connected computers that the **WWW** works on. You can think of the Internet as the roads that connect cities together. The **Web** comprises all the buildings that you see along the roads. The vehicles are the data moving from place to place, or from one computer to another.

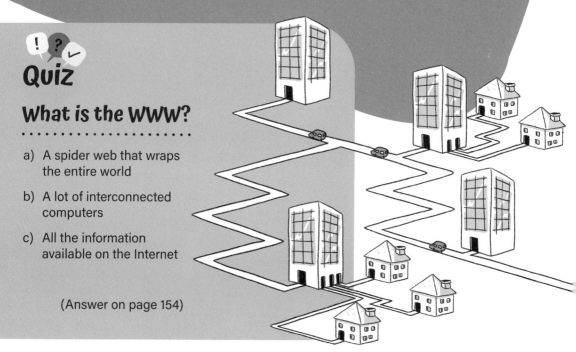

Quiz

What is the WWW?

a) A spider web that wraps the entire world

b) A lot of interconnected computers

c) All the information available on the Internet

(Answer on page 154)

You recognise your exhausted Cheepy from far away. Your poor friend is still fleeing from the cat. You follow them into a nearby building where a big sign reads: **antimatter** factory. It sounds like an interesting place, doesn't it?

"Animals and visitors are not allowed here!" someone shouts.

"Soooooo sorry," you apologise while running towards Cheepy.

Go to page 126.

Epil🌐gue

All the characters met at the CERN restaurant and shared their incredible stories. They exchanged contacts and promised to keep in touch.

How about a little prize for me?

Then, the tourist kept on travelling around Switzerland and France.

Mr Hacktosis revealed that instead of appreciating his creative genius, people had always been unwelcoming to him; he was furious and wanted revenge. The police were not convinced: they sent him to jail, and gave him a good toothpaste and toothbrush. His bad breath never disappeared, but one day, Mr Hacktosis completely vanished. The guards believe that he used his toothbrush to dig a hole in the wall of his prison cell and the toothpaste to hide the hole.

Cheepy took lessons from the animal trainer, Leonie, to learn to speak and fly higher. He is almost there, but he needs a bit more confidence.

The researcher continued to explore the mysteries of the Universe, on a slightly tidier desk.

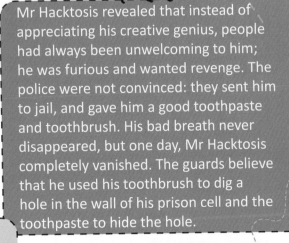

And the happiest of all was the student...

The story went on more or less in this way:

"Everybody is waiting for you at the auditorium," says Loris with an excited look on his face. "Really?" you are surprised and thrilled at the same time. "Yes, let's run there!" he enthuses.

At the auditorium, you are invited on stage where the CERN Director-General is facing the microphone ready to give a speech.

"We would like to commend you for facing the dinosaur so bravely!" the Director-General announces and presents a certificate to you.

Certificate

awarded to

‗‗‗‗‗‗‗‗‗‗‗‗‗‗‗‗‗
(Write your name above.)

for displaying invaluable curiosity, outstanding determination and impressive courage.

The rewards are:

An official invitation to come again to CERN anytime;

An unlimited order of
Galette des rois from the CERN restaurant;

The colossal 3-metre-high, 9-metre-long dinosaur.

Everybody claps, making the auditorium **vibrate** with excitement.

"Wow! Thank you sooo much," you say while shaking hands with the Director-General.

"You can learn to programme this **dinosaur**," suggests Loris. "For example, you can programme it to do backflips, to bark like a **dog**, or even to write your homework. Let your great imagination run **wild**."

"This is super ultra awesome!" you exclaim.

BEEEEEP BEEEEEP BEEEEEP

"Hi, Mum and Dad! Perfect timing! You won't believe what just happened: I got a big award here at CERN," you enthuse.

"Fantastic!" say your parents.

"It comes with a really, really **BIG** reward, but it can be used for school projects. Can I bring it home, please?" you ask impatiently.

"Of course! We are so proud of you," says your mum.

"I will inform your teachers immediately," adds your dad.

"I guess it's a deal," you say triumphantly. You have a feeling that the travel back home won't be as boring as your long ride to CERN.

"It can roar as well!" you say.

"Your prize can ROAR! ?!"

Answers and Solutions

Page 7

Answer: a). The average distance between the Sun and the planet Jupiter is 778 million kilometres!

Page 8

Answer: a) The largest scientific instrument; b) the most powerful **particle accelerator**; d) the highest man-made temperature ever reached; e) the first proof of the existence of a **particle** called **Higgs boson**.

CERN researcher's mission...

Page 46

Answer: c). One day, some physicists had a bet where the loser of a darts game would have to insert the word "penguin" in a scientific publication. These publications are important for researchers, but the loser played the game. He did not know how to use the word "penguin" in the text of the publication, but designed a diagram shaped like a penguin and published it. Every straight and wavy line of the penguin represents a **particle**. This intriguing way of visualising **particles**' transformations with lines was invented around 1950 by Richard Feynman, an American physicist.

Page 47

Answer: a). In the past, physicists loved looking at the traces left by microscopic bubbles. The bubble chambers were containers filled with liquid. When **particles** coming from space passed through this liquid, they created visible **tracks** of bubbles along the **particles**' path. Cameras mounted around the chamber captured the results. Some types of **particles** travel in a straight line, others curl into clockwise or anticlockwise spirals. That's a great way to visualise the invisible **particles** and their properties, but modern **detectors** have surpassed these bubble chambers by far. Stay tuned to learn more about them.

Page 90

Ms Alignment Genius is the lady who holds a mug with the letters "AG".

Continue your adventure on page 106.

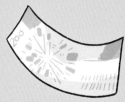

Page 114

Answer: a) A **particle** collision

Page 109

Answer: B. The wire has to be properly attached to both the positive (+) and negative (−) poles of the battery, otherwise **current** will not flow through the wire. The more wire you wrap around the nail, the stronger your **electromagnet** will be.

Page 61

Byte – a word

Kilobyte (~1000 bytes) – a page

Megabyte (~1,000,000 bytes) – a book or a photo

Gigabyte (~1,000,000,000 bytes) – an encyclopedia

Terabyte (~1,000,000,000,000 bytes) – a video lasting 500 hours

Petabyte (~1,000,000,000,000,000 bytes) – a HD video lasting 13.3 years

THE HIGHEST ARTIFICIAL TEMPERATURE INSIDE
ALICE DETECTOR (GUINNESS WORLD RECORD)
= 5.5 TRILLION °C (9.9 TRILLION °F)

HOT

TEMPERATURE OF A STANDARD
FREEZER = -20°C (-4°F)

TEMPERATURE OF A LIGHTNING
BOLT = 30,000°C (54,000°F)

THE COLDEST TEMPERATURE
EVER RECORDED IN ANTARCTICA
= -89.6°C (-129°F)

TEMPERATURE OF THE SURFACE
OF THE SUN = 5,500°C (9,930°F)

TEMPERATURE OF THE
LHC = -271°C (-456°F)

TEMPERATURE AT WHICH LIQUID WATER
BECOMES ICE = 0°C (32°F)

THE LOWEST
POSSIBLE
TEMPERATURE
= -273.15°C
(-459.67°F)

HIGHEST RECORDED TEMPERATURE ON
EARTH (DEATH VALLEY, US) = 56.7°C (134°F)

COLD   TEMPERATURE OF OUTER SPACE
= -270°C (-454°F)

Page 17

Page 75

The lines form the number 114.

Page 30

Answer: a). Plastic, food and gold
are not magnetic. Aluminium is
not attracted to the **magnet**, but
it interacts with a strong moving
magnet.

Page 15

Answer: C. Free **quarks** and free
gluons are the ingredients of the
primordial soup.

The temperature of the primordial
soup was too high for **atoms** to
form.

152

Just after the **Big Bang**, water did
not exist, and you can forget about
vegetables and broth.

A	T	L	A	S	T	Q	R	G	N	O
T	C	T	O	E	O	U	U	O	P	A
G	E	C	N	P	A	U	R	A	E	T
P	W	G	E	S	H	T	P	R	R	E
P	A	A	O	L	C	Y	O	C	L	K
M	E	N	L	E	E	T	S	C	M	N
G	I	N	L	I	C	R	I	I	O	S
D	L	E	G	E	C	T	A	T	C	B
C	E	U	T	U	R	E	O	T	C	S
N	A	E	O	A	I	R	T	H	O	Y
O	D	T	P	N	P	N	L	N	E	R

Page 23

The 17 remaining letters form the
sentence: GO TO PAGE TWENTY-ONE.

Page 23

The rule is to swap the first and last letters of each word.

Eakt eht dhirt rettel fo eht dorw shysip.
—→ Take the third letter of the word physics.

The third letter of the word "physics" is Y.

Page 21

Answer: a)

HEPY	HEYP	HPEY	HPYE	HYEP	HYPE
EHPY	EHYP	EYHP	EYPH	EPHY	EPYH
PHYE	PHEY	PEHY	PEYH	PYHE	PYEH
YHPE	YHEP	YPHE	YPEH	YEHP	YEPH

WRAAAAA

Page 85

It is the letter P.

Page 124

Answer: b). Finally, Prof. Virtualli's password is: CHEEEEEEEEEEEPY:-P

The tourist's trip...

Page 97

73	9	18	60	19	90	9	45	63
18	33	19	54	37	63	75	26	47
22	53	37	27	15	36	61	89	55
12	55	86	36	28	18	54	63	90
93	89	45	43	37	72	11	78	9
58	72	29	82	53	9	66	58	63
27	66	77	98	74	81	59	44	54
36	90	81	9	43	27	45	9	18

Page 96–97

Answer: c). The **protons** with the green and red lines collide inside the CMS **detector**.

Page 66

Answer: B.

Page 67

Answer: a) **Higgs boson**

Page 76

The right materials for the eruption are: vinegar, baking soda (bicarbonate of soda), dish soap, red food colouring, and an empty bottle.

Page 32

Page 147

Answer: c)

Option (b) is the Internet and option (a) is just a joke.

The student's quest...

Page 57

China – 茄子 (Qie zi, eggplant, which sounds similar to "cheese")

Finland – Sano muikku (Say vendace, a type of fish)

France – Ouistiti (it means marmoset, a monkey species)

Germany – Spaghetti

India – Paneer (an Indian cheese)

Iran – سیب (sēb, which means apple)

Italy – Formaggio, cheese

Japan – はい，チーズ (Okay! Cheese!)

Norway – Appelsiini (it means orange)

Serbia – Ptičica (p-tee-chee-tsa, it means little bird)

South Korea – 김치 (kimchi, a traditional dish made of fermented vegetables)

Spain – Patatas (potatoes)

Page 102

Page 59

Answer: f)

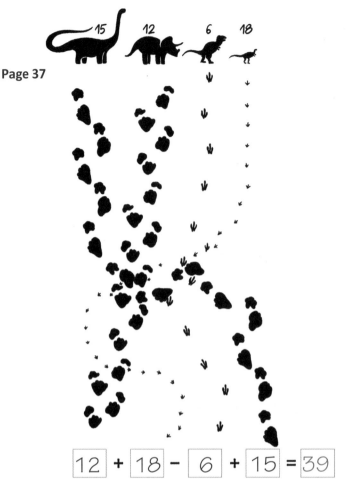

$$\boxed{12} + \boxed{18} - \boxed{6} + \boxed{15} = \boxed{39}$$

Go to page 39 to continue your adventure.

Page 38

The main difference is the **charge**. Matter and **antimatter** have opposite **charge**. **Protons** are positive, while anti**protons** are negative. **Electrons** are negative, while anti**electrons** (positrons) are positive. The three anti**quarks** are also different from the three **quarks**. Researchers are looking for other more subtle differences between matter and **antimatter**.

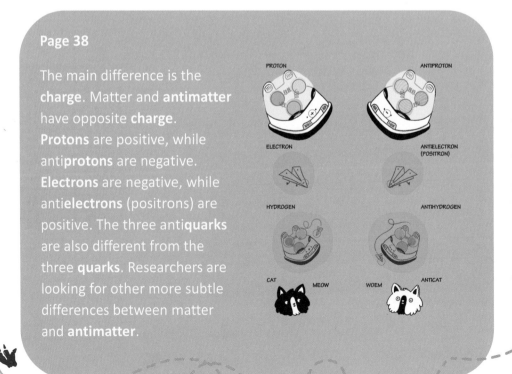

Page 43

Each letter of the alphabet matches with a number.

L: 5 + 2 = 7

H: 48 ÷ 8 = 6

C: 56 - 47 = 9

b: 3 x 3 = 9

The last two digits of the code which correspond to 'C' and 'b' will point you to page 99.

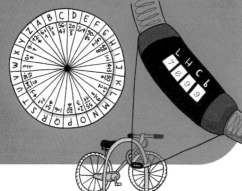

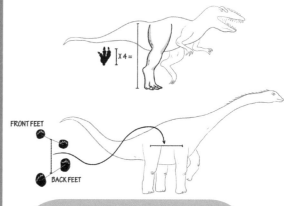

FRONT FEET

BACK FEET

Page 88

Brachio – arm; Cera – horn; Dino – terrible; Diplo – double; Docus – beam; Ptero – feather or wing; Raptor – robber; Rex – king; Saur – lizard; Tri – three; Tyranno – tyrant; Veloci – speedy

Page 87

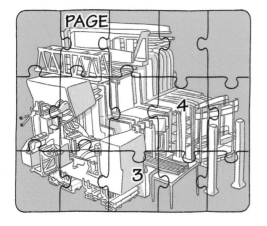

PAGE

GO TO <u>PAGE 3 4</u>.

Page 34

Answer: a). Applying $E=mc^2$, you find that 4 million tonnes of matter are transformed into a lot of energy. The energy released by the Sun every second corresponds to one million times the amount of energy that the entire world uses in a year.

Page 83

The intruders are a T-Rex, a brontosaurus and a bird.

Page 40

Answer: c). You do not need to travel too far to encounter some **antimatter particles**. Bananas release one anti**electron** about every 75 minutes.

How to make a chocolate accelerator
The adventure continues on the table: Bon Appétit!

Curiously CERN

The **LHC particle accelerator** is made up of more than 1200 superconducting **magnets** that bend the direction of the **particles**. Most of them have been painted in blue, so they look like huge blue tubes. If you could look inside these tubes, you would see an engineering marvel, including two pipes where **protons** fly through, and other components to keep the **magnets** very cold and under vacuum.

- 100 grams of soft butter

- 50 grams of cacao powder

- 300 grams of dried biscuits (cookies)

- Blue sugar icing

- Hollow wafer sticks

- Sugary sprinkles or colourful vermicelli

- 50 tonnes of Swiss chocolate... just kidding, 50 grams is enough!

Let's replace the pipes with two hollow wafer sticks and the rest with a delicious chocolate filling. You will need:

1. Mix together the soft butter, the cacao, the melted chocolate and the biscuits reduced to little crumbs. You can start by mixing them, first with a spoon, and then with your hands.

2. Give it a long and slim shape, like a salami, and fit the wafer sticks (the ones commonly used as ice-cream decorations, similar to the Russian *Trubochki*; alternatively, some cookie sticks will also be good) in the middle. Then put it in the fridge for 30 minutes.

3. Roll out the blue sugar icing and use it to cover the "salami".

4. Finally, fill the wafer sticks with some sugary sprinkles or vermicelli, which represent the **protons** that fly almost at the **speed of light** inside the pipes.

5. If you can resist the temptation, store the sweet **accelerator** in the fridge for 30 minutes before serving. The sweet "**particles**" will pop out of the tubes when you cut the cake.

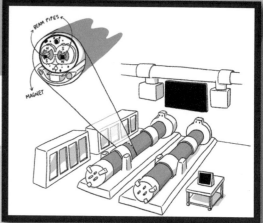

Tip: Build your own **LHC** tunnel with little bricks.

Dinosaur on the menu
Eat the dinosaur before it eats you

Science Byte

The Ginkgo biloba, a "living fossil"

It is not one of the ingredients of the recipe, but this plant, also known as maidenhair tree, is one of the oldest living tree species in the world, dating back to the **Jurassic** period. Its large seeds drop to the ground in autumn and emit a smell similar to rancid butter.

- 500 grams of potatoes
- 100 grams of olives
- Some pieces of medium Cheddar cheese
- Tomatoes or other vegetables for decoration
- A **dinosaur** egg (if you haven't got one, then 5 chicken eggs will do)

1. Peel the potatoes and boil them.

2. Blend the olives in an electric blender, but put one or two olives aside for decoration.

3. Cut the potatoes into small chunks and mix them with the eggs, the blended olives and the cheese pieces. Then cook the mixture on a big pan until it is done on both sides. Here you have the face of the **dinosaur**.

4. Now cut out a triangle for the mouth and decorate it with sharp teeth made of medium Cheddar cheese. Use the remaining cheese and olives for the eye and nostril: give it a dreadful look!

Tip: Add a slice of red pepper for the dinosaur's tongue so its face will look even angrier and hungrier.

Useful links

Would you like to visit CERN, the biggest particle physics institute in the world?

Visit CERN museums and reserve a place on the guided tours at https://visit.cern; or ask your teachers to book a visit for your entire class.

Do also check out the website of the new CERN Science Gateway project: https://sciencegateway.cern

Do you want to explore the longest sauropod tracks in Dinoplagne®?
You can find more information at https://www.dinoplagne.fr

Do you want to see a lot of animals at the largest natural history museum in Switzerland?

Do not miss the Natural History Museum of Geneva (*Muséum d'histoire naturelle de Genève*). Visit www.museum-geneve.ch

Schrödy's Glossary
Particle physics words and others according to your feline companion

Do you need help with any strange words? Ask me!

ACCELERATOR
A machine to speed up **particles**, and then... smash them into each other! Why? Humans are a really weird species, they want to 1) discover new **particles**, 2) understand how the Universe works, and 3) recreate the conditions that existed just after the **Big Bang**. CERN's biggest accelerator is the **Large Hadron Collider (LHC)**.

. . . .

ANTIMATTER and ANTIPARTICLES
"Anti" in front of a word indicates contrast. For example, antiparasitic collars protect cats from fleas and ticks. Similarly, anti**particles** are **particles** with the opposite **charge**. Since **protons** are positive, anti**protons** are negatively **charged**. **Electrons** are negative, so anti**electrons** (also called positrons) are positively **charged**. Get the idea? Bits of antimatter are all around us, but they do not last very long: as soon as an anti**particle** meets a **particle**, the two destroy each other leaving a puff of energy behind. A gram of antimatter that comes in contact with matter could cause a terrible explosion, like a bomb. That's why science-fiction movies love this stuff! However, these movies are based on fiction (!). It would take CERN millions of years to produce this amount of antimatter at the current production rate.

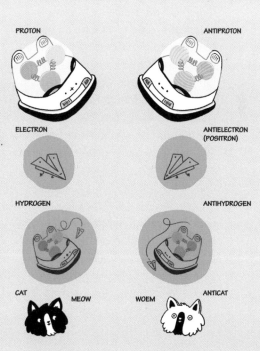

PROTON   ANTIPROTON

ELECTRON   ANTIELECTRON (POSITRON)

HYDROGEN   ANTIHYDROGEN

CAT   MEOW   WOEM   ANTICAT

ATOM

Matter is made of atoms. Almost everything on Earth is made of atoms. Water? Yes, it is made of two atoms of **hydrogen** and one atom of oxygen. Air? Yes, it is made of atoms, mostly nitrogen and oxygen. The most important thing in the world: cat food? Yes, it is made of atoms too.

BIG BANG

The Big Bang theory explains how the Universe began: around 13.8 billion years ago, the Universe was as small as a point, then it expanded to the current size, and it is still growing. The Earth is "only" about 4.5 billion years old. Anyhow, the Universe used to be a really boring place until the ancestors of cats and other feline species arose about 10–11 million years ago.

CHARGE

(as in, positive and negative charge)
An electric charge is a property of certain **particles**. For example, **electrons** have a negative charge and **protons** have a positive charge. **Particles** with the same charge repel each other, whereas **particles** with opposite charges attract one another. Stay away from humans who want to rub balloons or styrofoam peanuts against your fur! You may think that they want to cuddle you. Instead, they will make a fool of you: when someone rubs an inflated balloon on your fur, some **electrons** of your fur move onto the balloon. The balloon becomes negatively charged, and your fur positively charged. Now, when the balloon comes close, the fur is attracted to the balloon.

CURRENT
A stream of **electrons** flowing together.

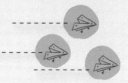

DARK ENERGY
This is still a big mystery. Dark energy is thought to make up a seriously large percentage of the Universe: something like 68 percent! It makes the Universe expand, but nobody knows what it is. If you find out, you will get a **Nobel Prize**, for sure! When you do, please tell everybody that you learnt about **particle** physics in Schrödy's Glossary. You will make me very happy and proud!

DARK MATTER
Dark matter is thought to make up about 27 percent of the Universe. But where is it? Nobody has sniffed it out yet. If you find it, you will become famous!

DETECTOR
Humans love photos, and sometimes they go nuts. Detectors are like super cameras that take 40 million pictures of **particles** per second. **Protons** crash inside the detectors and the resulting **particles** leave some **tracks** behind. The **LHC** is connected to four detectors: **ALICE, ATLAS, CMS** and **LHCb**.

DINOSAUR
Dangerous animals of the past. Dinosaurs lived between 245 and 66 million years ago and went extinct, but some are still alive today: the birds.

DOG
Terribly dangerous animal of the present. Actions to take: 1) run away, 2) look disappointed when humans cuddle them, and 3) protect your food, because dogs are so bad, they might eat it.

DOSIMETER
Instrument for measuring radiation, such as X-rays and gamma rays.

ELECTRON
Electrons are negatively **charged particles** that can be found in a cloud around the **nucleus** of **atoms**. They are responsible for electricity, magnetism and lightning too.

ELECTROMAGNET

Humans are an annoying species. They came up with all sorts of instruments to disturb cats' sleep: vacuum cleaners, washing machines, tumble dryers, food blenders, dishwashers, hairdryers, etc. Well, all these instruments contain electromagnets. These are **magnets** that work only when the electricity is turned on.

GLUONS

Gluons glue the **quarks** together. They are often represented as little corkscrews.

HIGGS BOSON and HIGGS FIELD

Cats hunt delicious preys, like birds and mice, but humans are a strange species... They like hunting bison, pardon me, bosons, like the Higgs bosons. It took humans more than 50 years to find these **particles**. But what's all the fuss about? Higgs bosons explain how all the elementary **particles** got their mass. The Higgs boson is connected to the Higgs field—don't think about fields for crops or grasslands for sheep. Don't ask me why, but humans also use the word "field" to indicate an invisible field of energy that fills all the space in the Universe. It sounds eerie, but it's not. The most important thing is that without the Higgs field, all **particles** would rush through space, you would have no **atoms** or **molecules**, and cats wouldn't even exist!

HYDROGEN

Hydrogen is the most abundant element in the Universe and the simplest **atom**: it has only one **proton** and one **electron**. It is found in stars, like the Sun. On Earth, hydrogen is found in the greatest quantity in combination with oxygen to make water.

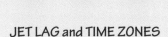

JET LAG and TIME ZONES

When it is daytime in your country, it's night-time at places on the opposite side of the Earth. For example, when cats in Switzerland are ready to go to sleep, kangaroos in Australia are having breakfast, and llamas in South America are enjoying an afternoon snack. For this reason, the world is divided into 24 different time zones: one for each hour of the day. If you take a flight from Europe to Australia, you travel rapidly across time zones, but the body cannot adapt so quickly. As a result, after you've landed at your destination, you might feel tired during the day and have trouble sleeping at the right time. This disruption of your body clock is known as jet lag.

JURASSIC

This term refers to a period of time between 200 million and 145 million years ago marked by an abundance of **dinosaurs** as well as the first appearance of birds and mammals. The Jurassic era gets its name from the Jura Mountains at the border between France and Switzerland, where limestone strata from the period were first identified.

LHC – LARGE HADRON COLLIDER

CERN's biggest **accelerator**, the LHC, is an engineering marvel, a "freezer" and a racing circuit for **protons**... all in one!

- "Large" because it is 27 kilometres (17 miles) long: the biggest **particle accelerator** ever built so far.
- "Hadron" because it accelerates **protons**, which belong to the hadron family.
- "Collider" because the **protons** smash at four collision points: ALICE, ATLAS, CMS and LHCb.

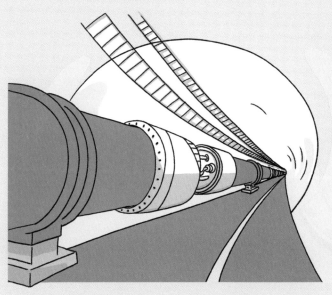

MAGNET and MAGNETIC FIELD

Some humans use magnets to stick notes on the fridge and some are nice enough to write "Buy cat food" on those notes. So you see, magnets can be useful. They always have a North pole and a South pole, and they can attract or repel objects made of certain materials. The area around the magnet, where other objects feel the push away from the magnet or the pull towards the magnet, is called a magnetic field. The Earth is like a very big, but weak, magnet: the invisible magnetic field of the Earth can be detected with a magnetic compass! Magnets also exert an invisible force on **charged particles**. For example, **LHC** magnets can bend the paths of **protons** without touching them.

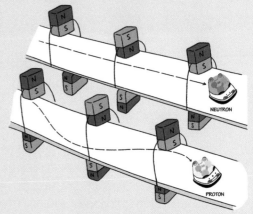

MOLECULES

Atoms can join together to form molecules.

MUON

The big cousin of the **electron**. It is also negatively **charged**.

NEUTRON

It is a **particle** made of **quarks** and **gluons**, like the **proton**; but while **protons** are positively **charged**, neutrons are neutral. Both **protons** and neutrons are parked in the **nucleus** of an **atom**.

NOBEL PRIZE

When Alfred Nobel, the inventor of dynamite, passed away in 1896, he decided to leave his wealth for awards given in his name. The prestigious Prizes still exist and they are awarded to people who have done outstanding studies and made significant contributions to society.

NUCLEUS

It is the centre of an **atom** and is made of **protons** and **neutrons**. In the case of **hydrogen**, the nucleus only has a single **proton**.

....

PARTICLE

A particle is a tiny little thing. If you want to be cool, you need to distinguish between elementary and non-elementary particles. Nothing to do with elementary school in North America... Elementary particles cannot be broken down into smaller pieces. By definition, particles have mass but no volume. They are basically points, but they have been given a bit of shape in this book, otherwise you wouldn't be able to see them on the page. While my ancestors and I have been busy discovering new mouse holes, humans have discovered a lot of particles. In this book, you encounter only some of them: **gluons**, **quarks**, **electrons**, **muons**, **photons** and **Higgs bosons**. **Protons** and **neutrons** are also called particles, but they are not elementary particles because they contain **gluons** and **quarks**.

....

PARTICLE PHYSICS

The science that deals with **particles**.

PHOTOELECTRIC EFFECT

The photoelectric effect allows humans to transform light into electricity, which takes place in solar panels.

PHOTON – Particles of light

Hats off to this **particle**. Cheetahs are the fastest animals, but photons are unbeatable: they whizz around at the **speed of light** through a vacuum and just a bit slower through any gas, liquid, or solid. Photons are the most abundant **particles** in the Universe and they are massless, which means they do not interact with the **Higgs field**.

PROTON

Positively **charged particles** located in the **nucleus** of all **atoms** together with **neutrons**. They are made of **gluons** and **quarks**. Humans built a huge machine called the **LHC** to accelerate **protons** at a mind-blowing speed of almost 300,000 kilometres per second.

QUARKS

You can find quarks inside **protons** and **neutrons**. Interestingly, there are six types of quarks and humans have given them super funny names: up, down, top, bottom (or beauty), charm and strange. They also come in three varieties depending on a property known as "colour". The colour can be red, green or blue; but quarks are not really painted like confetti. **Particles** called **gluons** "glue" the quarks together.

QUANTUM PHYSICS

This subject studies the really weird behaviour of **particles** and related phenomena. It was okay, until a physicist called Schrödinger came up with silly ideas about zombie cats that are half dead and half alive. Luckily, it was just a thought experiment. (See page 69.)

SPEED OF LIGHT

Light travels very, very, very fast. The speed of light in a vacuum is around 300,000 kilometres per second (186,000 miles per second). **Protons** inside the **LHC** dart at a speed that is pretty close to the speed of light.

STANDARD MODEL OF PARTICLE PHYSICS

Cats have a standard list of all the delicacies in the Universe, but humans have come up with a set of laws that describe all the known **particles** and forces in the Universe: the Standard Model of particle physics. The model works, but it does not explain **dark matter** and other unsolved mysteries.

TRACKS

You can identify animals by spotting their tracks on snow, mud and sand. **Particles** are super-duper tiny and invisible, but when they enter the **detectors** they also leave some tracks behind. The tracks give information about the **particles'** speed, energy, direction and **charge**.

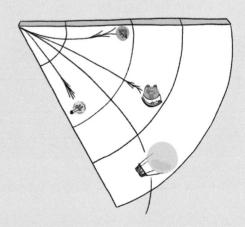

WORLD WIDE WEB (WWW)
Every smartphone can access the World Wide Web (WWW). The World Wide Web allows you to find information, share photos with friends and shop online. It is also the best place to find photos and videos of cute cats!

Final notes

- Although a lot of dinosaur footprints were found in the Jura Mountains, the soil was not suitable for bone fossilisation.
- Some liberties were taken in representing the meat-eating dinosaur.
- The characters in this book are fictitious; any resemblance to real people, cats or cockatiels is purely coincidental.
- Just in front of CERN data centre, a shelter for computer mice was built some years ago as an April Fool's stunt to raise awareness on computer attacks. It reminds everybody not to click on untrustworthy links and websites that can hide computer viruses.

Acknowledgements

Writing this book was such a fantastic adventure. I was very fortunate to be accompanied by a lot of incredible companions, friends and colleagues.

Thank you to CERN Director-General Fabiola Gianotti, CERN education, communications and outreach group, CERN librarian Tullio Basaglia, the leader of the High-Luminosity LHC project Lucio Rossi and CERN-devoted physicists Maria and Giuseppe Fidecaro for their supportive messages and inspiration.

Thank you to Dinoplagne® Scientific Advisor Pierre Hantzpergue for introducing me to the dinosaurs of the Jura Mountains.

Thank you to Arnaud Maeder, Hervé Groscarret, Andreas Schmitz and Laurent Vallotton from the Natural History Museum of Geneva for telling me the fascinating stories of the most interesting specimens.

Thank you to the members of The Ogden Trust for promoting physics education starting from a young age.

Thank you to the World Scientific Publishing team, in particular Ruth Wan, Daniele Lee, Claire Lum, Amanda Gwee, Jimmy Low, Lionel Seow, Serene Ng and Elena Nash. A very big and special thanks to Charmaine Weng – the editor that every writer for children's books wishes to work with.

Thank you to the illustrator Claudia Flandoli for her drawings that bring the adventures to life.

Thank you to my family for giving me sparkling strength. This book is dedicated to my little, techy niece, who loves Schrödy and will soon be able to play with him.

Thank you to all my friends for all the wonderful discussions about books, science and culture. A special thanks to my friends Prachi and Serhat for all the conversations about particle physics.

Thank you to Josh Goh, the first child who read the draft of the book and wrote some lovely comments to me.

And thank you to all the readers of *Your Adventures at CERN*:
I hope you enjoy the adventure and keep on exploring the beauty and mystery of science!

About the Author

Letizia's childhood was laden with gamebooks, action films and Japanese animations. Nothing, however, could beat the amazement she felt at the age of 8 when she came close to a real T-Rex skeleton. Over the years, she has immersed herself in the world of science, received a PhD in Biochemistry from the University of Cambridge (UK), and kept her enthusiasm for adventure and exploration. Secretly, she still has a soft spot for paleo-creatures.

She loves writing about the latest discoveries, making videos about scientists, exploring science museums and taking part in science festivals. During her time at CERN, she had special access to the biggest particle accelerator on Earth, and the experimental caverns 100 metres underground. She thought CERN was a wonderful setting for a gamebook that introduces the fascinating world of particle physics. She hopes this book will inspire young readers to be intellectually intrepid.

About the Illustrator

When Claudia was a child, she dreamed a lot of what she'd be when she grew up: a scientist! No wait, a cartoonist! Why not an illustrator? Or perhaps a… cat lady?

We can happily report that she managed to become a little bit of each: a cartoonist who writes and draws about science. Since 2015, she has published several comics and a graphic novel, and has created illustrations for biomedical research journals. Making the illustrations for this book helped her with the final piece of the puzzle: one of the main characters is… a cat! Wonderful!

Instructions for the back cover game

Find some friends, a die and playing pieces. (You can also cut out the playing pieces provided at the bottom of the next page.) Players take turns in a clockwise order; highest throw of the die goes first, starting from **1** (CERN Globe of Science and Innovation).

- If you land on **4**, dart to **10** at the speed of light.

- If you land on **7** (the invention of the World Wide Web), **12** (a lucky four-leaf clover) and **19** (Einstein), move forward three spaces.

- If you land on **14**, go back to **2**.

- If you land on **16**, open the book to a random page and add up the digits of the page number. If the sum is an even number, go to **17**; if it is odd, go to **32**. For example, if you randomly opened the book and land on page 56, and 5 + 6 = 11, an odd number, you move to **32**.

- If you land on **21**, swing to **30**.

- If you land on **23**, the waterjet of Geneva's famous fountain, *Jet d'Eau*, brings you up to **25**.

- If you land on **26**, escape by moving back to **25**.

- If you land on **27**, follow the dinosaur tracks back to **22**.

- If you land on **33**, go back to **28**.

- The first player to reach **34** (the end) wins! (Note: You can only win by rolling the exact number needed to land on **34**.)

Have fun!

Cut-outs

You may use these cut-outs to play the games or complete the activities in this book.

Page 67
(Particle Sudoku)

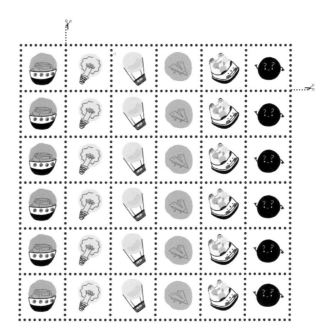

Page 113
(CERN access card)

Page 80 and
Back cover
(Board game pieces)

Published by

WS Education, an imprint of
World Scientific Publishing Co. Pte. Ltd.
5 Toh Tuck Link, Singapore 596224
USA office: 27 Warren Street, Suite 401-402, Hackensack, NJ 07601
UK office: 57 Shelton Street, Covent Garden, London WC2H 9HE

British Library Cataloguing-in-Publication Data
A catalogue record for this book is available from the British Library.

Photo credits:
P29: Erik Gustafson (https://commons.wikimedia.org/wiki/File:Pauli_wolfgang_c4.jpg),
"Pauli wolfgang c4", marked as public domain, more details on Wikimedia Commons:
https://commons.wikimedia.org/wiki/Template:PD-old
P103: Credit: Portrait of Marie Curie and her daughter Irene. Welcome Collection. Attribution 4.0
International (CC BY 4.0)

YOUR ADVENTURES AT CERN
Play the Hero Among Particles and a Particular Dinosaur!

ISBN 978-981-123-490-3 (hardcover)
ISBN 978-981-123-558-0 (paperback)
ISBN 978-981-123-491-0 (ebook for institutions)
ISBN 978-981-123-492-7 (ebook for individuals)

Editor: Charmaine Weng
Design and layout: Lionel Seow

Printed in Singapore